JAMIE MAXWELL is a Scottish political journalist. He has contributed to *New Statesman*, *The Sunday Herald* and *The Scotsman*, and is currently on the editorial team of *Bella Caledonia*. Over the last two years he has been heavily involved in editing and publishing his father Stephen Maxwell's books *Arguing for Independence* and *The Case for Left Wing Nationalism*. He is currently working on a book of the collected essays of Tom Nairn.

DAVID TORRANCE is a writer, journalist and broadcaster, regularly appearing on the BBC, Sky and STV to talk about politics and the constitutional debate. He has a column in *The Herald* every Monday and has also written or edited around a dozen books on Scottish history and politics, including an unauthorised biography of the First Minister, *Salmond: Against the Odds*. He is currently based in Edinburgh but has also lived in London for long periods.

SCOTLAND'S REFERENDUM

A Guide for Voters

JAMIE MAXWELL AND DAVID TORRANCE

Luath Press Limited

EDINBURGH

www.luath.co.uk

First published 2014

ISBN: 978-1-910021-54-5

The paper used in this book is recyclable.
It is made from low chlorine pulps
produced in a low energy, low emissions
manner from renewable forests.

Printed and bound by
CPI Group (UK) Ltd, Croydon, CR0 4YY

Designed by Tom Bee

Typeset in 10.5 point Din
by 3btype.com

The authors' right to be identified as
author of this work under the
Copyright, Designs and Patents Act 1988
has been asserted.

Contents

Preface

One inevitable side effect of the referendum debate has been the publication of a plethora of books on almost every aspect of independence: for and against, its implications in economic and cultural terms and even its spiritual dimension. This is, of course, a good thing. At the same time, however, there remains a gap in the literature – a straightforward, non-biased voters' guide to the independence referendum.

We hope this short book fills that gap. It is deliberately concise and balanced. Our aim was to provide a primer for each of the main issues surrounding independence, as well as to accurately represent the views of those on both sides of the debate. There is of course much more that could be said about everything we address, but the 'Recommended Further Reading' chapter provides options for more in-depth analysis and/or polemic.

There is an understandable (yet at the same time unrealistic) desire for 'facts' in the referendum debate, but just as the creation of a new state produces uncertainty so too does remaining part of an older one. All that can reasonably be presented is what each side believes will happen following either a YES or NO vote; it is for each voter to work out for themselves which position is more credible and, indeed, desirable.

Hopefully *Scotland's Referendum: A Guide for Voters* will make that task a little easier.

Jamie Maxwell, Journalist and Writer
David Torrance, Associate Director, Five Million Questions
June 2014

Five Million Questions

Understanding Scotland's Referendum

The Five Million Questions project at the University of Dundee has been an expression of the core purpose of Scottish universities. As repositories of knowledge, analysis and, we hope, some measure of wisdom if we were not to make especial effort to engage the public in informed debate at this moment then when would we do so at all?

Since the autumn of 2012 the project has engaged many thousands of those charged with the responsibility of voting in the referendum in September 2014. We have done so through lectures, debates, seminars, exhibitions, interviews and a plethora of online activity across many, if never possibly all, the subject areas that will be touched by Scotland's decision.

The role in this debate of academics and the universities they populate has been at times controversial. In some part that has been due to a misunderstanding of the role of academia. Funded by the taxpayer, our academics are not the journalists of the BBC (themselves too frequently accused of favour from either side – but that is not for here). Academics should abhor bias but they are not practitioners of studied neutrality. If evidence leads you to a conclusion then you have the freedom to state it. In many cases, and this may well be one given the profundity of the question at hand and the huge uncertainty surrounding us, you have a duty to state that conclusion.

We hope that our project has been something of a safe space in a debate that has, at times and by acclaim, been deemed too febrile to best serve our needs. That is how we view this book and why we have been eager to support it. Two excellent writers well versed in the case at hand bringing their personal analysis to bear. You may not agree with either perspective and you may even feel it is short on the hard fact 'answers' that many people are demanding of either side. Over the past two years we have become aware that the only editorial line of Five Million Questions has become the explanation that you are not going to get many of the answers you are looking for. This is a job of interpretation, analysis, synthesis and conclusion that falls to all of us. The answers you reach will vary but we do hope this book will help. The Five Million of course refers to the population of this ancient country. Not all that number have a vote or will use it. But everyone deserves to be considered and as many as possible should be heard and allowed, in some hope of an answer, to put their question.

Michael Marra, Director
Five Million Questions, University of Dundee

Introduction 1

The Road to 2014

1

Referendums on Scotland's constitutional future are no longer a novelty to Scots of a certain age. On 18 September 2014, anyone born after 1961 (more than half its current population) will be answering YES or NO to a question about self-government for the third time.

The first, on 30 March 1979, asked if voters wanted a devolved 'Scottish Assembly' based in Edinburgh, and although a slim majority answered YES, a controversial stipulation in the 1978 Scotland Act said it would only happen if more than 40 per cent of the total electorate (rather than those voting) assented. What many saw as an historical wrong was finally righted on 11 September 1997 when Scots were asked two different but related questions – did they agree there 'should be a Scottish Parliament' and should it have tax-varying powers? The result was 'yes-yes' by a significant majority.

In that context, the writer Neal Ascherson views the 2014 referendum as 'little more than the third putting of the same question' – should Scotland govern itself? But in fact at the third time of asking there is an important difference – whereas in 1979 and 1997 Scots were being asked about the 'devolution' of power from Westminster, this time they will be asked to say YES or NO to complete (with certain qualifications) independence from the UK Parliament in London.

This is often referred to by supporters of independence as 'self-determination' or the 'sovereignty of the Scottish people', although it could be argued that both concepts have existed at least for the past 35 years. Since 1979 the UK government has accepted that constitutional change can only happen with the assent of a majority of those resident in Scotland. This choice has, to an extent, been available to Scots since the Scottish

National Party (SNP) started contesting elections in 1935, and particularly so since the late 1960s when the party – the chief driver of the 'National Movement' for Scottish independence – first became a major force. It is just that Scots self-determined in favour of the Union.

And that, of course, is a reminder that the independence debate is not a new phenomenon. It has been around – to varying degrees – since Scotland first joined England (and Wales) to form a new state called 'Great Britain' following the 1707 Treaty of Union. Over the next few hundred years pro-independence sentiment came and went. When, for example, Great Britain joined Ireland to form the 'United Kingdom' in 1801, it is probably safe to say that most Scots were content to be part of the UK, but towards the end of that century when agitation for 'Home Rule' (or devolution) in both Ireland and Scotland began to gather support, the dynamic began to change.

It is important to remember that few Scots until after the Second World War actually desired full independence for Scotland, rather they argued for devolution, Home Rule or 'Dominion status' (like Canada or Australia) within the UK and the then British Empire. For example the 'Scottish Covenant', reportedly signed by two million Scots in the early 1950s, demanded a devolved Scottish Parliament sitting in Edinburgh. By the time a solicitor called Winnie Ewing won the Hamilton by-election in 1967, however, all that had changed – the SNP's goal was very much independence.

Ewing's victory was short-lived and she lost her seat at the 1970 general election, but in 1974, when two further elections were held in February and October, the SNP had its electoral breakthrough, winning seven and eleven seats respectively, but, more significantly, around 30 per cent of the popular vote (opinion polls at the time put support for independence at similar proportion of the Scottish electorate). The 'Unionist' parties – between 1974 and 1979 Labour was in government – responded by legislating for a devolved Assembly in Edinburgh and although this fell far short of what the SNP actually wanted, the party still campaigned for a YES vote in 1979.

The government of James Callaghan had not intended to hold a referendum at all, but a group of backbench MPs opposed to Scottish devolution successfully amended the relevant legislation so that voters had to be consulted before an Assembly came into being. And when, as mentioned above, the number of Scots voting YES failed to reach 40 per cent of the electorate, the first government of Margaret Thatcher (elected in May 1979) was able to repeal the 1978 Scotland Act.

It was not a good election for the SNP, which lost 9 of its 11 MPs, and for roughly the next decade successive Conservative governments at Westminster resisted calls for devolution from various groups in Scotland, including the Campaign for a Scottish Assembly (later Parliament), the Labour Party, the SNP and others. But after the number of Conservative MPs in Scotland dropped to just ten following the 1987 general election, pressure grew much greater, even more so when the SNP gained Govan at a 1988 by-election. At this point three political parties – Labour, the Liberals (later Liberal Democrats) and the SNP – joined forces with Scotland's churches, trade unions and other 'civic' organisations to form the Scottish Constitutional Convention (the SNP later withdrew on the basis that the Convention refused to consider independence).

The Scottish Constitutional Convention sat in Edinburgh for the next few years, delivering its blueprint for a Scottish Parliament – elected by proportional representation – shortly before the 1992 general election which many believed would result in a Labour government and therefore a Scottish Parliament. The SNP was also riding high, with one opinion poll even showing that a majority of Scots supported independence. Unexpectedly, the Conservatives gained a fourth term with a small majority and, although it promised to 'take stock' of how Scotland was governed within the UK, devolution was still ruled out as an option (the SNP had increased its vote by seven per cent but gained only three MPs). Meanwhile cross-party campaigns such as 'Scotland United' continued to agitate for a Scottish Parliament based in Edinburgh.

Only following the 1997 election, when Tony Blair's New Labour party won a landslide victory over John Major's Conservatives, did constitutional reform become a reality. Within weeks a White Paper called 'Scotland's Parliament' had been published and on 18 September it was overwhelmingly endorsed in a referendum. As all the Scottish parties prepared to contest the first elections to the Scottish Parliament in May 1999 (including the Conservatives, who had lost all their MPs north of the border), several opinion polls showing rising support for independence, and although the SNP (led since 1990 by an MP called Alex Salmond) got almost 29 per cent of the vote, the first Scottish Executive (the devolved government) was a Labour-Liberal Democrat coalition.

In the mid-1990s, Labour's then spokesman on Scotland, George Robertson, had famously predicted that devolution 'would kill independence stone dead' and, at least initially, that appeared to be an accurate forecast – at the 2003 Scottish Parliament election the SNP's vote fell to just 24 per cent and in elections to the European Parliament the following year the party got less than a fifth of the popular vote. John Swinney, leader of the SNP since 2000, resigned and Alex Salmond, who had surprised everyone with his resignation four years previously, returned to the fray.

Initially, the SNP leadership team of Salmond and Nicola Sturgeon made only a modest impact (Salmond was still an MP rather than an MSP), but when Scots went to the polls for the third time in 2007 there was a perfect political storm – Labour had been in government (with the Lib Dems) for eight years and had also been damaged in Scotland by the Iraq War, while the SNP appeared to be a different party, more positive in outlook and full of ideas. The mood of many Scots was that they deserved a shot at running Scotland's devolved government.

The result was a close run thing – Labour and the SNP were neck and neck in terms of the popular vote, but as the last results came in the latter pulled ahead and became the largest party in the Scottish Parliament by just one seat. After negotiations with the Liberal Democrats came to nothing Alex Salmond became First Minister of a minority Scottish Executive (quickly rebranded the 'Scottish Government'). But although the SNP had increased its support (as it did again four years later) it was not matched by rising support for independence – opinion polls continued to show only around a third of Scots in favour.

The SNP had changed its policy on how independence would be delivered several years earlier. From the 1970s onwards it maintained that negotiations would begin once it had gained a majority of either Scottish seats in the House of Commons (reduced to 59 at the 2005 UK election) or in a devolved Scottish Parliament, but in 2000 it switched to a referendum policy – in other words, even if the SNP gained a majority it would still consult the Scottish electorate before beginning moves towards independence.

At the 2011 Holyrood election, ironically, the SNP gained precisely that – a majority of seats in the Scottish Parliament – and a referendum, which it had pledged at the last two elections, suddenly became a realistic prospect. It is fair to say the SNP did not expect to win a majority and had been deliberately vague about when a ballot might be held. There was also a legal difficulty – the Scottish Parliament's powers did not include conducting referendums on constitutional issues, for those were 'reserved' to the Westminster Parliament.

Again the dynamic shifted relatively quickly – in early 2012 the Prime Minister, David Cameron, offered the Scottish Government temporary powers to hold an independence referendum. But there were caveats – it could only consist of one question and had to be held by the end of 2014. Throughout most of that year Westminster and Holyrood thrashed out the details, finally reaching a deal in October when the 'Edinburgh Agreement' was signed. There had been much haggling over the question to be asked, but that too had been resolved – 'Should Scotland be an independent country?'

How is Scotland currently governed?

2

2

Like most nations, Scotland is governed at various different levels – 32 local authorities, a devolved Parliament based in Edinburgh, the UK Parliament in London and the institutions of the European Union in Brussels and Strasbourg all make decisions that affect voters' day-to-day lives. These layers of government are, of course, inter-related, but it breaks down roughly as follows:

Brussels

The European Union (EU) is a partnership of 28 Member States of which Scotland (as part of the UK) has been a member since 1973. It is based on a series of international treaties, signed and approved by all EU Member States, the most recent being the Lisbon Treaty that came into force in December 2009.

The day-to-day functioning of the EU is governed by a series of institutions. These include the European Parliament (to which Scotland sends six Members), the European Commission (its executive body) and the Council of the European Union (sometimes called the Council of Ministers). EU institutions are responsible for making laws that apply across all Member States, and the UK is represented in all of these institutions.

Once a law has been agreed at EU level it normally has to be implemented by national governments. In the UK, this means a law is implemented by the Scottish Government in the case of devolved matters, and by the UK Government in the case of reserved matters. EU laws covering, for example, international trade, foreign policy, consumer protection, energy and employment are the responsibility of the UK Government as these are reserved matters.

But EU laws dealing with devolved matters such as agriculture, fisheries, the environment, justice and legal affairs are the responsibility of the Scottish Government. In these cases, Members of the Scottish Parliament (MSPs) are responsible for scrutinising the Scottish Government's implementation of European law.

The EU has developed a 'single market' through a uniform system of law (interpreted by the European Court of Justice in Luxembourg) that applies in all 28 Member States. As part of the UK, however, Scotland is neither part of the Schengen Area (under which 22 EU Members have abolished border controls) nor the 'euro' single currency used by 18 Member States (and administered by the European Central Bank in Frankfurt).

Meanwhile the Committee of the Regions, an assembly of local and regional representatives, provides devolved parts of Member States (such as Scotland) with a direct voice in the EU's institutional framework, although its actual power is limited. The Scottish Government also has a European Union Office (SGEUO) based in Brussels which supports its work on EU policy and relationships with EU institutions, including 'UK Rep', the UK's Permanent Representation to the EU, of which Scotland forms a part.

(Separately, Scotland – as part of the UK – is a signatory to the European Convention on Human Rights, an international treaty to protect human rights and fundamental freedoms in Europe.)

Westminster

Since the 1707 Treaty of Union that formed 'Great Britain' in place of Scotland and England, both have been represented – along with Wales and (Northern) Ireland – at the Westminster

Parliament in London. Then as now Parliament meets at the invitation of the monarch, who is the hereditary and therefore unelected head of state. Originally Scotland had just 45 MPs lthough this was later increased to 72. Under the terms of the 1998 Scotland Act, however, this was reduced to 59 prior to the 2005 general election. Elections to the House of Commons now take place every five years.

Each MP represents a territorial 'constituency' in the House of Commons, which is elected under a system called first-past-the-post. And although the Scottish Parliament now controls most domestic policy (see below), the UK government – comprising MPs and Members of the House of Lords – still deals with 'reserved' matters such as foreign affairs, defence, the economy, monetary policy, broadcasting, energy, inter-national development and welfare. Representing Scotland in this respect is a Secretary of State for Scotland, who sits in the Cabinet, and a small department called the Scotland Office (from 1885 until 1999 this was called the Scottish Office, and had much more power than at present). Among the House of Commons' Select Committees is one covering Scottish Affairs, which scrutinises the UK government's functions in relation to Scotland.

At the 2010 general election the Labour Party won 41 Scottish constituencies, the Liberal Democrats 11, the SNP 6 and the Conservatives just one. The SNP often points out that under what it refers to as the 'Westminster system' Scotland can often end up being governed by a UK administration that a majority of Scottish voters did not vote for – ie during the period of Conservative government from 1979 to 1997 when no more than 22 Tory MPs (and after 1987 half that number) were returned in Scotland. Of course this can go the other way, so between 1997 and 2010 Labour had a majority of MPs in both Scotland and the UK as a whole.

Scotland is also represented in the Upper House of the UK Parliament, the House of Lords. Until 1999 this comprised a mix of hereditary (inherited) and 'life' (appointed) peers, but at that point all but 92 hereditaries were expelled, meaning the current House of Lords is predominantly appointed. There are currently around 800 members, many of whom are Scottish, although it is difficult to say exactly how many because they do not represent geographical constituencies. The House of Lords scrutinises legislation approved by the House of Commons (the Lower House) and can amend Bills, although it is not allowed to prevent them becoming law. Until 2009 the Upper House also acted as the highest court of appeal in the UK (though not for Scottish criminal cases), a function now fulfilled by a Supreme Court also situated in Westminster. Of its 12 'Justices', two are generally specialists in Scots Law.

Holyrood

Since 1999 the Scottish Parliament, often referred to as Holyrood, has been the law-making body for devolved matters in Scotland. In addition to passing legislation its Members (MSPs) – like MPs in the UK Parliament – also debate topical issues and hold ministers, including the First Minister (currently Alex Salmond), to account. Every person resident in Scotland is represented by eight MSPs – one constituency member and seven elected via eight 'regional' lists, although both sorts of MSPs have equal status at Holyrood.

2

Elections to the Scottish Parliament used to take place every four years although since 2011 this was increased to five to avoid clashing with UK Parliament elections. Again, as at Westminster, the Scottish Government is formed by the party (or parties) with the most seats in the Scottish Parliament, and its main role is to formulate and implement policies in devolved areas. Occasionally Westminster will legislate on devolved matters if it has permission to do so (a 'Legislative Consent Motion', often referred to as a 'Sewell Motion') from the Scottish Parliament.

Under the terms of the 1998 Scotland Act, devolved powers include agriculture, education, health, housing, law and order, sport and the arts, tourism and economic development, and many aspects of transport such as rail and roads. The Scottish Parliament's fiscal powers are more theoretical than real. From its creation it has had the ability to vary the basic rate of income tax up or down by three pence, although to date no government has chosen to do so. The 2012 Scotland Act, meanwhile, gave MSPs the ability to control ten pence within each income tax band (as well as borrowing powers), although this does not take effect until 2015/16.

The same legislation also devolved control over stamp duty, land tax, landfill tax, air guns and speed limits, while giving Holyrood a role in appointing Scottish representatives to the Crown Estate and BBC Scotland.

Several 'subject' committees, meanwhile, scrutinise legislation produced by the Scottish Parliament and take evidence from a wide range of witnesses. Other committees, like that dealing with Public Petitions, allow members of the public to directly influence the legislative process.

Local Government

The Scottish Parliament is also responsible for Scotland's 32 local authorities, all of which are governed by a 'council' consisting of elected councillors elected every four years. The largest Scottish council is Glasgow (with more than 600,000 inhabitants) and the smallest is Orkney (with fewer than 20,000). Most councils are members of the Convention of Scottish Local Authorities (COSLA), a sort of lobbying group through which the Scottish Government usually engages with leading councillors.

Each council elects a leader, while a Provost or Lord Provost (in the case of Glasgow, Edinburgh, Aberdeen and Dundee) acts as a figurehead, and is responsible for providing a range of local public services, including education, social work, housing, libraries, waste management, policing, fire and rescue, arts and culture, licensing, parks, leisure centres and transport.

Elected volunteers also form around 1,200 Community Councils in Scotland. They bridge the gap between local authorities and the communities they represent, expressing the views of local areas to the relevant council and other public bodies.

Should Scotland be an independent country?

The Case for YES

3

Democracy is central to the YES campaign's case for independence. Scottish voters have rejected six of the 11 governments elected at the United Kingdom level since 1970. The current UK Government is a coalition of two parties – the Conservatives and the Liberal Democrats – which between them secured just 12 Scottish seats out of a possible 59 in Scotland at the 2010 general election. By contrast, at the same election, Labour took 41 seats. Under independence, the SNP and its allies say Scotland would be guaranteed governments that reflected the preferences of the Scottish electorate, thereby correcting the 'democratic deficit' it suffers as part of the UK.

YES campaigners also argue that independence would also enable Scotland to modernise and enhance its democratic institutions. They claim the UK's political system – which includes the House of Lords (one of the largest unelected legislative chambers in the world) and an unwritten constitution built around the principle of absolute parliamentary sovereignty – is outdated. With independence, Scotland could replace the House of Lords with an elected upper chamber or, alternatively, stick with Holyrood's current unicameral system. Scotland could also have a written constitution which, like the most advanced constitutions, identifies the people as the ultimate source of political authority and enshrines in law a clear set of civil, political and social rights for each Scottish citizen. Without the constraints of a written constitution, recent UK governments have been free to pass various pieces of authoritarian legislation. The most notable example of this was in 2005, when the Blair government passed a law allowing terror suspects to be held for up to 28 days without charge.

The SNP argues Scotland is well-quipped to become a succ-essful independent country, pointing out that, in recent years, Scotland has had lower levels of debt and a smaller deficit than the rest of the UK, and has generated more tax per head of the population than the rest of the UK for the each of the last 30 years (*Scotland's Future*, 2013). The party contends that Scotland's economy has failed to achieve its potential within the Union. It highlights that Scottish economic growth rates have lagged behind growth rates in many comparably sized European countries for the last five decades. According to YES Scotland, between 1977 and 2007 Scottish growth aver-aged 2.3 per cent per year, while growth among small inde-pendent European states such as Denmark, Finland and the Netherlands averaged 2.8 per cent per year.

One of the defining themes of the SNP's economic case for independence is Westminster's 'mismanagement' of North Sea oil. Between 1976 and 2011, total North Sea oil tax revenues amounted to £285 billion, of which Scotland's share – accor-ding to a median line division of North Sea territory – was £257 billion. Over the same period Norway enjoyed a parallel oil boom – and saw its per capita GDP rise from 9 per cent below that of the UK to 71 per cent above it. Conversely, the SNP says successive Westminster governments have 'squan-dered' Scottish oil revenues. Instead of investing them in Scotland's public and industrial infrastructures or building up a Norwegian-style sovereign wealth fund, they have used them to finance day-to-day expenditure. Oil revenues were wasted most egregiously during the 1980s, when Margaret Thatcher spent record oil tax returns on rising welfare bills

– a consequence of her attempts to control inflation through heavy redundancies in the public and manufacturing sectors.

An independent Scotland, on the other hand, could use the remaining 40 years' worth of North Sea oil to improve its economic infrastructure.

YES campaigners cite Scotland's poor social record (one of the worst in Western Europe) as evidence that Westminster is failing Scotland. In 2007, the Federation of Small Businesses (FSB) published a report indicating that Scotland had the lowest life expectancy of any country in the OECD, as well as some of the most severe health inequalities. Meanwhile, the Child Poverty Action Group (CPAG) estimates that one in five Scottish children live in poverty – compared to just one in ten Danish and Norwegian children. The SNP says Scotland's poverty crisis is being compounded by a combination of public spending cuts and welfare reforms imposed by a UK government that lacks widespread support among Scottish voters. For the YES campaign, Scotland needs full control over its fiscal and welfare policies in order to address its chronic social problems. At a minimum, the higher revenues generated by a more dynamic Scottish economy could be reinvested in public services, benefitting those low-income Scots who rely on those services most.

The YES campaign acknowledges that some form of 'devolution-max' or fiscal autonomy would represent a significant improvement on the current constitutional settlement but insists Scotland needs full independence to set its own course in international affairs. Many in the SNP and across the independence movement, such as the Scottish Socialist Party (SSP), believe successive Westminster governments have the made the wrong foreign policy and defence choices for Scotland. They argue an independent Scotland would not have participated in the 2003 invasion of Iraq, nor would it have chosen to station a huge concentration of nuclear weapons less than an hour north of Scotland's largest city. YES campaigners anticipate that, with independence, Scotland would play a constructive role in international peace-keeping efforts, lead the way in the drive against global nuclear proliferation and rebuild its relationship with the European Union in the wake of England's flirtation with EU withdrawal.

Another key theme for the YES campaign is immigration. YES campaigners say the two main Westminster parties are engaged in a race to the bottom over immigration, competing with one another to drive away prospective migrants. They claim this has had a negative impact on Scotland's economic and social development, pointing to that fact that, under London control, Scotland's population is ageing at the same rate as the rest of the UK's but growing at just half the rate. By contrast, they say, an independent Scotland could develop an immigration system that suited Scottish economic needs and, in the process, benefit from the advantages that come with increased cultural diversity.

YES campaigners accept a YES vote in September will not be a cure-all for Scotland's ills, and that Scotland will still face an underperforming economy, gross inequalities of wealth and a burgeoning demographic crisis after independence. They insist, however, that it is only with the powers of independence that Scotland will be able to tackle these challenges and take full responsibility for its own future.

Should Scotland be an independent country?

The Case for NO

4

As with the case *for* independence, those who argue that Scotland should remain part of the UK do so for a variety of reasons. The Labour Party, for example, stresses 'solidarity' with people living in England, Wales and Northern Ireland, the Liberal Democrats have a vision of a more federal UK of which Scotland would be a part, while Conservatives argue that Scotland has more influence internationally as part of the UK.

The formal cross-party NO campaign, Better Together, has summarised this in what it calls 'a simple notion' – Scotland has 'the best of both worlds', in the sense that it has a devolved Scottish Parliament with a wide range of powers but also representation in the UK Parliament and the opportunity to play a role in UK-wide organisations and institutions. For example, several Scottish MPs have become Prime Minister (most recently Gordon Brown) as well as senior Whitehall civil servants and Cabinet ministers.

A big part of the pro-UK argument (as is true of the contrary case) is economic. Better Together argues that as well as being part 'of one of the biggest economies in the world' Scotland also benefits from higher public spending per head than the UK average, about £1,200 per person per year, which comes to Scotland via a 'block grant' spent by the Scottish Government and Parliament. They also point out that Scotland's biggest export market is England and the rest of the UK, to which Scottish firms sell twice as much as they do to the rest of the world combined. Scots, meanwhile, can live and work wherever they want to in the UK without worrying about different employment laws or tax regimes.

And while the NO campaign acknowledges that Scotland could be an economically-viable independent nation, it also emphasises what it sees as the risks associated with being so, arguing that at present Scotland shares 'risks and rewards' with the rest of the UK. For example when it comes to currency, the three Unionist parties have all argued that if Scotland becomes independent then it would not be able to retain sterling (as the Scottish Government claims). Therefore, warns Better Together, Scotland would have to set up its own currency or adopt the Euro, resulting in higher mortgage and interest rates, and higher borrowing rates as a result of instability in global financial markets. They also argue that Scottish fuel bills are lower by virtue of a UK-wide energy market that gives Scotland a high level of subsidies for renewable fuels.

Another strand of the argument against independence is that Scotland currently has more global influence and 'impact' as part of the UK. As such, argues Better Together, Scotland is a permanent member of the United Nations Security Council and has 270 embassies and consulates around the world helping Scottish companies and travellers. Within the European Union, it adds, Scotland also punches above its weight as part of the one of its largest Member States. Similarly, Scotland and the UK sit at other international 'top tables' such as the World Trade Organisation, G8, NATO, etc. It also warns that joining the EU and NATO as a newly independent nation might not be as easy – or indeed as quick – as supporters of independence suggest.

When it comes to defence, opponents of independence argue that the UK Armed Forces 'are the best trained in the world' and that Scotland currently benefits from an Army, Navy and Air Force larger than it could afford as an independent country. In terms of international aid, meanwhile, Better Together points to one of the largest programmes (as a proportion of GDP) in the world, partly administered from premises in East Kilbride and widely respected for its role in helping the poorest parts of the world and providing specialist help following natural or man-made disasters.

Although most public services in Scotland are already under the devolved control of the Scottish Parliament, NO campaigners make the point that when it comes to the National Health Service (NHS) Scots continue to benefit from 'cost-free, hassle-free access' to specialist – and often lifesaving – treatment anywhere else in the UK, something it suggests might not be possible if Scotland became independent. And in terms of higher education, Better Together argue that Scotland's universities benefit from being part of a UK network, not least in terms of research funding, of which Scottish institutions receive a bigger UK share than population would justify.

Pro-Union campaigners have also deployed a more emotional argument against independence. In a speech delivered in Edinburgh in early 2012 David Cameron said it was 'a question of the heart as well as the head'. 'The United Kingdom is not just some sort of deal, to be reduced to the lowest common denominator,' he said. 'It is a precious thing; it is about our history, our values, our shared identity and our joint place in the world. I am not just proud of the Union because it is useful. I am proud because it shapes and strengthens us all.' The Prime Minister also argued that far 'from growing apart', Scotland and England were actually 'growing together'. 'There are now more Scots living in England, and English people living in Scotland, than ever before,' he said. 'And almost half of Scots now have English relatives.'

Opponents of independence often use the British Broadcasting Corporation (BBC) as a symbol of these cultural bonds. As Better Together has argued, Scottish licence fee payers contribute about £300 million to the BBC but get around £3.6 billion worth of programmes – both television and radio – in return. They suggest that an independent Scotland, like the Republic of Ireland, would have to pay a fee to use catch-up services like iPlayer while paying a higher licence fee for fewer programmes and more commercial advertising.

More generally, Better Together suggests that the SNP and broader YES Scotland campaign is guilty of attempting to have their cake and eat it, by implying that an independent Scotland could preserve certain aspects of being part of the UK – for example its currency, energy market, university research funding and even a sense of 'Britishness' – while shedding others. 'It isn't credible,' they say. 'The facts don't support it.'

4

Which parties and campaign groups support independence?

5

Business for Scotland

Business for Scotland was set-up by six Scottish business owners and directors to articulate the business and economic case for an independent Scotland. It describes itself as 'a neutral business and economic policy think tank' and claims to have more than 1,300 members. It publishes articles and analysis highlighting the strengths of the Scottish economy. Its chief spokesmen are Gordon MacIntyre-Kemp and Ivan McKee. Earlier this year, Business for Scotland successfully forced the Confederation of British Industry (CBI) to register as a formal member of the NO campaign in light of the public and financial support it had given to Better Together. A number of high-profile CBI members subsequently left the organisation, leading the CBI to reverse its official support for Better Together.

> **Becoming an independent country means Scotland's economic future will be in Scotland's hands, and that business and economic policies will be tailored to improving productivity and growth, within the distinct Scottish business and economic landscape.**
> *– From the Business for Scotland Declaration*

National Collective

National Collective was founded in 2011 by a group of Edinburgh-based writers and artists. It is as a 'non-party movement for artists and creatives who support Scottish independence'. It's various branches across the country organise local events emphasising the 'cultural advantages' of independence. It now boasts more than 2,000 members, including a number of high-profile writers and performers such as Alan Bissett and singer Lou Hickey. In 2013, National Collective became embroiled in a legal battle with Vitol, a major oil trading company, after it published an article linking Vitol executive and Better Together donor Ian Taylor to a Serbian war criminal. National Collective subsequently altered the content of their article and Vitol dropped its legal challenge.

> **We support independence because of the opportunity that comes with the ultimate creative act – creating a new nation. And we believe that to get there, we need to inspire and engage the people of Scotland in a way that has never been seen before.**
> *– National Collective*

Radical Independence Campaign (RIC)

The Radical Independence Campaign was set-up in 2012 to act as a left-wing counterweight to the official YES campaign. Its first conference, held in Glasgow in November 2012, attracted nearly 1,000 delegates and hosted a range of speakers, including Robin McAlpine of the Jimmy Reid Foundation and Isobel Lindsay of Scottish Campaign for Nuclear Disarmament, as well as a number of foreign speakers. Its second conference, in November 2013, attracted nearly 1,200 delegates. RIC has organised a series of mass canvassing sessions in low-income areas as part of a campaign to get low-income Scots registered on the electoral roll. It was established by a group of young, Glasgow-based socialist activists but now has branches across the country.

> **We are against austerity. We want a modern republic, one not tied to the monarchy. We oppose discrimination, Trident and nuclear weapons. We think these are very**

YES ✕ appealing ideas and could contribute towards strengthening the vote for an independent Scotland.

– RIC organiser, Jonathan Shafi

Scottish Campaign for Nuclear Disarmament (SCND)

SCND is committed to the abolition of Britain's nuclear deterrent as a step toward the global elimination of nuclear weapons. It is independent of British CND. In September 2012 its membership voted to formally support, and campaign in favour of, independence.

> **The independence referendum provides a great opportunity not just to remove Trident from Scotland, but to achieve nuclear disarmament in Britain. People will consider a whole range of subjects when deciding how to vote in 2014. We recognise that we have members who will not be supporting independence for other reasons. On the issue of nuclear disarmament, our advice is to vote YES.**

YES ✕

– Chair of SCND, Arthur West

Scottish Green Party (SGP)

The Scottish Green Party began life as the Scottish branch of the UK Green Party but became a fully independent political party in 1990. It has had representation in the Scottish Parliament since 1999. In 2003 it won seven Holyrood seats but lost five of them at the subsequent 2007 election. It had two MSPs elected in 2011. The SGP is left leaning and environmentalist. It has campaigned in favour of a Land Value Tax, the legalisation of same-sex marriage and against the construction of a second Forth crossing. In October 2012, the Party voted to formally affiliate to YES Scotland. It is critical of the SNP's defence proposals and supports an independent Scottish currency.

> The debate which Scotland has embarked upon is about far more than whether decisions should be made at Westminster or Holyrood. We have the opportunity to ask ourselves what kind of country we want to live in, what kind of society we want to build, and what kind of economy we want to run.
> – SGP co-convenor, Patrick Harvie MSP

Scottish Independence Convention (SIC)

The Scottish Independence Convention was launched in 2005 as a cross-party platform to campaign for an independence referendum. It has party affiliates, including the SNP and the SSP, as well as non-party affiliates. Its governing council of 16 members is elected annually. It has no formal policy programme but it has produced various pieces of literature arguing for independence.'

> The role of the Scottish Independence Convention has changed. We were founded to deliver a referendum. That battle's now been won. Our role now is to be creative and engage as wide an audience as possible in the discussion about the future of our country and what we mean by sovereignty.
> – SIC convenor, Elaine C. Smith

Scottish National Party (SNP)

The Scottish National Party was formed in 1934, following the merger of the National Party of Scotland and the Scottish Party, with the aim of winning electoral support for an independent Scotland. It secured its first Westminster seat in 1945 but lost it again at the 1950 election. It had no parliamentary representation up until 1967, when Winnie Ewing won the Hamilton by-election. Following a surge in its membership, the Party went on to secure 11 seats and 30 per cent of the Scottish vote at the second general election of 1974. In the 1979 election, after the defeat of the first devolution referendum, it lost all but two of those seats. The Party made little progress at Westminster during the 1980s and '1990s, but in 1999 won 34 seats at the first Scottish Parliamentary elections. It then fell back to 27 seats at the subsequent 2003 election. Its breakthrough came four years later, when it became the largest single party at Holyrood with 47 seats, beating its closest rival Labour by a single seat. In 2011 it won 45 per cent of the vote and a majority of seats – 69 – at the Parliament.

Today, the SNP describes itself as a 'moderate, left-of-centre European party'. It supports Scottish membership of the EU and of NATO. After independence, it argues that Scotland should go on using the Pound as its currency and says Scotland and England will continue to share a 'social union'.

In November 2013, the SNP launched its formal blueprint for an independent Scotland, *Scotland's Future: Your Guide to an Independent Scotland*. Among the key policy proposals outlined in *Scotland's Future* are:

i) The first government of an independent Scotland will be formed in May 2016 after the Holyrood elections that year

ii) By 2024, all children from the age of one will be entitled to full-time state-funded childcare of 1,140 hours per year

iii) The introduction of a points-based immigration system to encourage more migrants to Scotland.

The SNP is led by Alex Salmond. Its deputy leader is Nicola Sturgeon.

> [Scotland is] rich in human talent and natural resources. We are one of the wealthiest nations in the world. With independence, we can build the kind of country we want to be. People down the decades have wondered if a country blessed with such wealth, talent and resources could and should have done more to realise the potential we know exists for everyone. Those generations could only imagine a better Scotland. Our generation has the opportunity to stop imagining and wondering and start building the better Scotland we all know is possible. This is our country. This is Scotland's future. It is time to seize that future with both hands.
> – *SNP leader and Scottish First Minister, Alex Salmond*

Scottish Socialist Party (SSP)

The Scottish Socialist Party, a coalition of small left-wing groups, emerged ahead of the first Scottish Parliamentary elections in 1999, where it won a single seat. It went on to secure a further five seats at the 2003 Holyrood elections. The party split in early 2007 and lost all its MSPs at the election in May of that year. The remainder of the SSP campaigns alongside Yes Scotland under the slogan 'An Independent Socialist Scotland'. Its National Convener, Colin Fox, sits on the YES Scotland board.

> [The SSP] will continue to highlight the significant advantages Independence brings to Scotland; no more Tory

YES

Governments, no more Trident missiles, no more 'bedroom tax', returning the Royal Mail to public ownership, a fairer tax system, and above all self-determination for the people of Scotland at last – all in all a much more attractive prospect than the one we currently face.
– *SSP national convenor, Colin Fox*

Women for Independence

Women for Independence was set up in 2012 to try persuade more women to support independence. It is a grassroots network of campaigners and activists. It works in close conjunction with the official YES campaign, as well as with the main pro-independence parties and other pro-independence groups.

YES

I want women to be front and central in this debate. I want to hear what women up and down the country have to say and to hear their worries and their hopes. And I want to play my part in persuading other women, that not only is an independent Scotland possible, but that it's our best opportunity to realise our hopes and dreams for our families and communities.
– *Women for Independence campaigner, Jeanne Freeman*

YES Scotland

YES Scotland was established in 2012 as the official cross party platform to campaign for a YES vote in the referendum. It is an umbrella organisation encompassing a range of different political parties and groups, including the SNP, the Scottish Greens and the SSP. Its chief executive is the former BBC journalist Blair Jenkins and its chair is Dennis Canavan, a former Labour MP.

YES Scotland doesn't take formal policy positions, but it has built its campaign around a number of key themes, most notably social inequality in the UK and Scotland's economic potential. YES Scotland has established a series of local branches and interest groups which operate across Scotland. These include Trade Unionists for YES, Third Sector YES, Yes LGBT and Scots Asians YES.

> A YES vote is a rejection of Westminster politics and power and a preference for Scotland's future being in Scotland's hands. Scotland already has most of the structures in place for independent statehood. We are almost certainly better prepared for independence than any other European country pursuing self-determination in the last 100 years. We have the experience of devolution, great financial strengths and a clear transition process.
>
> – *YES Scotland chief executive, Blair Jenkins*

Which parties and campaigning groups oppose independence?

6

Better Together

Better Together is the official cross-party campaign to keep Scotland in the UK and achieve a NO vote on 18 September 2014. It is run by a coalition of senior politicians from Labour, the Liberal Democrats and Conservatives and is headed up by the former Chancellor Alistair Darling, a Scottish Labour MP. Figures such as former Prime Minister Gordon Brown, former Lib Dem leader Sir Menzies Campbell and former Scottish Conservative leader Annabel Goldie are also heavily involved.

Better Together launched on 25 June 2012 at Napier University in Edinburgh, shortly after the launch of YES Scotland (also in Edinburgh). Based in Glasgow (like Yes Scotland), its campaign director is a former Labour activist called Blair McDougall, who heads up a team of paid staff and the web campaigners Blue State Digital (which worked on President Obama's election campaign in the US). Unlike YES Scotland, the formal NO campaign does not take policy positions per se, emphasising that each of its component parties has its own views. But it is united in wanting Scotland to remain part of the UK.

Its website – bettertogether.net – says:

> We passionately believe the best choice for our future is to remain a strong and proud nation while benefiting from the security and opportunity we can take advantage of as part of a bigger United Kingdom. Devolution offers us the best of both worlds: we have a strong Scottish Parliament taking important decisions about schools, hospitals and jobs AND we benefit from the strength, security and opportunities we can take advantage of being part of a bigger United Kingdom. In these economically

uncertain times, Scotland has the absolute reassurance that comes from the financial back-up of being part of the United Kingdom.

Like YES Scotland, Better Together also acts as a campaigning umbrella under which specific groups such as Forces Together and Academics Together argue for Scotland to remain part of the UK from different policy perspectives.

The Scottish Labour Party

The largest party under the Better Together banner is the Scottish Labour Party – Scotland's largest political organisation for much of the post-war era. In Westminster elections it still dominates Scottish politics with 41 out of 59 MPs, although in the Scottish Parliament it is much weaker, with only 37 seats out of 129, enough for it to be largest opposition party. Under recent internal reforms the Glasgow MSP Johann Lamont now leads the whole party (rather than, as before, just its Holyrood group), while in the House of Commons MSP-turned-MP Margaret Curran is Shadow Secretary of State for Scotland. Her boss is Ed Miliband, the current leader of the UK Labour Party.

When the Labour movement first emerged as an electoral force in the early 20th century it was strongly committed to 'Home Rule' for Scotland, or devolution, although by the 1950s this pledge had been quietly shelved. As mentioned in Chapter 1, only when Labour came under pressure from the SNP in the 1970s did it revive its enthusiasm for a devolved Scottish Assembly or Parliament. Throughout the 1980s and 1990s, however, Labour was prominent in the devolution campaign and took an active part in the cross-party Scottish Constitutional

Convention that helped formulate plans for a Scottish Parliament. And when Tony Blair became Prime Minister in 1997, his government moved quickly to legislate for devolution to Scotland, subject to a referendum in September that year.

From 1999 until the SNP won the 2007 election, the Scottish Labour Party governed Scotland in coalition with the Scottish Liberal Democrats. Throughout this period it was, of course, opposed to independence, although in May 2008 the then Scottish Labour leader Wendy Alexander challenged the minority SNP Scottish Government to 'bring on' a referendum, arguing that if it brought forward a referendum bill (as it had promised to do by 2010) then Labour MSPs would vote for it.

Alexander was attempting to call Alex Salmond's bluff, confident he would either refuse, or agree and lose the referendum, but Gordon Brown (the then Prime Minister) appeared unconvincing in his support and within a few weeks – under pressure due to a row about her leadership campaign funding – she resigned as leader. Thereafter the party's stance on an independence referendum was unclear, although after the 2011 Holyrood election it supported the negotiations that led to the Edinburgh Agreement.

Having backed more powers for the Scottish Parliament via the cross-party Calman Commission after the 2007 election, in March 2014 Scottish Labour's own Devolution Commission also published a report called 'Powers for a Purpose', which recommended giving MSPs greater control of income tax (beyond the powers due to come in force in 2015/16), housing benefit and the ability to run Scotland's single rail franchise as a 'not for profit' company. Labour says it will legislate for these extra powers if it wins the 2015 general election at Westminster. But not all Labour voters are necessarily pro-Union – just as opinion polls suggest some SNP supporters will vote NO in the referendum, it is also likely some Labour supporters will vote YES.

The Scottish Conservative & Unionist Party

Also part of Better Together is the Scottish Conservative Party, officially known as the 'Scottish Conservative and Unionist Party', the 'Unionist' part of its name referring to Ireland rather than Scotland. Between 1912 and 1965 the party was known as the 'Scottish Unionists' because of its commitment to maintaining the Union between Great Britain and Ireland (after 1922 Northern Ireland). It was also strongly committed to maintaining the Union between England and Scotland, although during the 20th century it devolved significant 'administrative' power to Scotland, and built up a team of officials based at St Andrew's House in Edinburgh.

In 1968 the Scottish Conservatives also became the first mainstream UK party to pledge a devolved Scottish Assembly, although when the party won the 1970 general election this failed to transpire. When Margaret Thatcher became leader of the Conservative Party in 1975 she gradually phased out the devolution commitment and throughout her premiership (1979–90) the UK government was staunchly anti-devolution and, of course, opposed to independence.

Only after losing all its MPs at the 1997 general election (and the resounding referendum vote in favour of devolution) did the Scottish Conservative Party change its mind. It contested the first elections to the Scottish Parliament in 1999 and won

17 MSPs under an electoral system, ironically, its leaders had opposed. At the next few elections the Scottish Conservative share of the vote declined steadily but in 2011 it still won 15 MSPs.

Like the Scottish Labour Party, the Scottish Conservatives participated in the cross-party Calman Commission after the 2007 election, which recommended giving the Scottish Parliament control of ten pence within each income tax band, stamp duty and some other powers. And, like Labour, it has promised to devolve further powers in the event of a NO vote. Its devolution commission – chaired by the former Tory Leader of the House of Lords Tom Strathclyde – reported in early June and recommended that the ability to set all bands on income tax in full ought to be devolved to Holyrood, and also the ability to create 'supplementary' benefits, the general aim being to make the Scottish Parliament more responsible for the money it spends. Again, like Labour, Conservatives plan to legislate accordingly should it form a government after the next UK general election.

The Scottish Liberal Democrats

The third and final party in Better Together is the Scottish Liberal Democrats, perhaps the strongest and most consistent supporters of Scottish devolution. It was formed from a merger of the old Liberal Party and the short-lived Social Democratic Party (SDP) in the late 1980s and played an active part in the Scottish Constitutional Convention which considered what form devolution might take. Sir David Steel (later Lord Steel, the Scottish Parliament's first Presiding Officer) was the Convention's joint chairman.

But the Scottish Lib Dems often emphasise its much older support for a federal UK, or 'Home Rule all Round', ie devolution equally applied across the nations and regions of the UK. This policy was associated with the Liberal statesman William Gladstone, who (unsuccessfully) advocated Home Rule for Ireland in the late 19th century. In those days, the Liberals were a party of government, although a century on it is a much smaller electoral force, having won just five MSPs at the last Holyrood election in 2011 and 11 MPs for Scottish constituencies at the UK general election in 2010.

That said, since 1999 the Liberal Democrats have once again become a party of devolved and Westminster government. Between 1999 and 2007 it formed the devolved Scottish Executive with the Scottish Labour Party, while since 2010 it has been the junior partner in the UK Coalition government. But although consistently in favour of Scottish devolution (and indeed further powers), it was until 2011 not in favour of a referendum on independence. Indeed, the Scottish Lib Dems failed to form a coalition Scottish Government with the SNP in 2007 because it could not agree with Alex Salmond's desire for a vote on leaving the UK.

In 2012 the Scottish Liberal Democrats published a report called 'Federalism: the best future for Scotland' (2012), which set out its vision of a federal UK including additional fiscal (and other) powers for the Scottish Parliament, and in 2014 another report dubbed 'Campbell II' (the commission's chairman was Sir Menzies Campbell), which set out a timetable for implementing more devolved powers and, ultimately, creating a more federal UK.

Devo Plus

Set up by the centre-right think tank, Reform Scotland, and led by the former Lib Dem MSP (and Member of the House of Lords) Jeremy Purvis, Devo Plus (or devo+) campaigns for further devolution that would see the Scottish Parliament – as well as other parts of the UK – raising as much of the money it spends as possible. To that end, it promotes a detailed agenda including fiscal and welfare powers. And although it is officially non-party, its backers include former Holyrood Presiding Officer Alex Fergusson (a Conservative MSP), Tavish Scott (a former Scottish Lib Dem leader) and Duncan McNeill (a Labour MSP).

On its website – devoplus.com – the group says it provides:

> the best way forward for Scotland, offering a sustainable future for Scotland within the UK. It is not a compromise between independence and the status quo, and is more popular than both'. It also claims Scotland would be able to 'adapt to its unique circumstances, fulfil its potential and promote growth if it is able to raise as much as possible of its own taxation. Devo Plus will make both Holyrood and Westminster accountable and responsible for raising what each spends in Scotland.

Conservative Friends of the Union

Although part of Better Together, in March 2012 the Scottish Conservatives also launched Friends of the Union (CFU), designed to give Tory activists and voters a focal point for Conservative-themed campaigning in the run up to the independence referendum. At its launch, Scottish Tory leader

Ruth Davidson was joined by the then Welsh Secretary Cheryl Gillan, UK Conservative Party deputy chairman Baroness Warsi and former Ulster Unionist leader David Trimble to stress its pro-Union message.

By autumn 2012 the Scottish Tories claimed more than 50,000 people from across Scotland had pledged support for CFU, contributing donations amounting to almost £150,000. Despite its name, the party made clear that membership was open to all Scots and not just Conservative Party members. In September 2012 Ruth Davidson said: 'There is now a proper grassroots movement in place to stand up for those who want to prevent the break-up of the UK and I look forward to standing shoulder to shoulder with people from all walks of life and all parts of the country to preserve the Union.'

United with Labour

In May 2013 the Scottish Labour Party also launched its own standalone pro-Union campaigning group, United with Labour, at an event with former Prime Minister Gordon Brown. Reports suggested this had something to do with the unhappiness of some Labour activists and trade unions at having to campaign alongside Conservatives and Liberal Democrats under the Better Together banner.

United with Labour's website says: 'We define our politics by the values and principles of the Labour movement; solidarity, fairness, equality, community and social justice; values that are not remnants of the past but forces for good in the future.' It also looked to a future Scotland 'based on Labour values', adding: 'The referendum is the biggest decision the people of

Scotland will face for 300 years and it is important that we have strong Labour voices speaking for the majority of Scots who believe we are better working together with our neighbours in the United Kingdom.'

6

The Issues: Economics

Banks

In the autumn of 2008, Scotland's two largest banks, the Royal Bank of Scotland and Halifax Bank of Scotland, were handed bail-out packages by the UK Exchequer amounting to £37 billion. The banks faced insolvency as a result of the global financial crisis. The banks were subsequently given additional support by the UK government. The collapse of RBS and HBOS added a new dimension to the debate over Scottish independence – supporters of the Union argued that an independent Scotland would not have been able to afford the cost of the bail-outs, while nationalists said the failure of successive UK governments to properly regulate the financial industry illustrated Westminster's mismanagement of the Scottish economy. Experts disagree about how the cost of the bail-outs would have been divided had Scotland been independent in 2008. One view is that Scotland would have been responsible for providing most or all of the bail-out funds. Another is that the costs would have been divided according to the distribution of RBS and HBOS' operations across the British Isles. In March, Mark Carney, the Governor of the Bank of England, said there was a 'distinct possibility' that RBS would have to relocate to England if Scotland voted YES. This comment was made in reference to EU rules requiring a bank to headquarter in the country where it conducts the majority of its business.

What the Scottish Government / YES campaign says:

> **The contribution of an independent Scotland's taxpayers to any bank bail-out would have been the same as it has been with Scotland part of the UK. Eighty per cent of the peak losses at RBS stemmed from its London-based businesses. The financial crisis shows us that bailing out the**

banks – like reinsurance – is a risk that is globe in nature and shared between countries, and any tales about Scotland having to accept the burden all by itself are pure myth.

– *Business for Scotland chief executive, Gordon MacIntyre-Kemp,*

What the UK Government / NO campaign says:

If the UK Government had not acted when it did not only would RBS have collapsed with the loss of thousands of jobs, but Bank of Scotland would have gone out of business too. These were Scotland's two biggest companies and two iconic institutions woven into the fabric of Scottish life who only survived because Scotland is part of Britain and all the financial security that comes with being part of such a successful economic and social union.

– *Scottish Conservative MSP, Murdo Fraser*

Business

Scottish business does not speak with one voice on independence. While a string of major business figures, such as BP chief executive Bob Dudley and Shell boss Ben van Beurden, have expressed their support for the Union, a number of high profile business people, including Jim McColl of Clydeblowers and Brian Souter of Stagecoach, have come out in favour of independence. In February, a poll found that almost half of Scotland's small business owners believed independence would be bad for their businesses, compared to just ten per cent who said it would have no effect. However, YES campaigners point to the high levels of foreign direct investment in Scotland over recent years as evidence that the prospect of independence has not affected business confidence in Scotland. In April, employers' association the Confederation of British Industry (CBI) formally affiliated to the NO campaign, prompting the resignation of a number of its members, including the broadcaster STV and public bodies Visit Scotland and Scottish Enterprise. The CBI subsequently reversed its decision.

What the Scottish Government / YES campaign says:

> YES
>
> Scotland needs the powers to compete and competition is good for the UK economy. Independence should be seen as a catalyst for structural reform across the UK... A YES vote this year can be the trigger for major reform that will be in the long-term interests of London and the rest of the UK.
> – *Business for Scotland chairman, Tony Banks*

What the UK Government / NO campaign says:

> NO
>
> Being part of the UK is good for Scotland's economy. It secures thousands of jobs across the country and keeps down costs for families on mortgages, credit card bills, car loans and at the supermarket checkout. Leaving the UK means more costs, fewer jobs and cuts to public services. Recent warnings about the risks of separation from Scotland's largest employers make clear that independence would cost jobs for thousands of Scots.
> – *Better Together chairman, Alistair Darling*

Credit Rating

Sovereign credit ratings are used to indicate the level of risk attached to a country's capacity to repay its debts. A country is often given different credit ratings by different credit rating agencies. Currently, the UK has an AAA credit rating with Standard and Poor's (the highest possible rating) but AA+ rating with Fitch. Countries with low credit ratings, such as crisis-stricken Greece, face high borrowing costs when they look to borrow from international markets. Unionists warn that, with a large debt and fluctuating oil revenues, an independent Scotland would face a low credit rating and therefore high borrowing costs. Nationalists respond by pointing out that Scotland's overall level of debt is proportionately lower than that of the UK's, while its per capita GDP (including North Sea oil revenues) is higher. In February, Standard and Poor's said Scotland would qualify for its highest economic assessment, while Fitch has warned that Scottish independence could lead to a credit downgrading for the rest of the UK.

What the Scottish Government / YES campaign says:

> Standard & Poor's have concluded that Scotland's wealth levels 'are comparable' to those of AAA-listed nations, and that as an independent country Scotland will qualify for S&P's 'highest economic assessment'. That is a glowing assessment of the Scottish economy from an impartial source and completely demolishes the scaremongering of the NO campaign.
> – *Deputy First Minister, Nicola Sturgeon*

What the UK Government / NO campaign says:

> Credit rating agencies rate the UK as triple A. The low interest rates today of 1.8 per cent are a consequence of this. That helps Scottish firms with their borrowing costs, and Scottish households with their mortgage costs. A

one per cent increase in interest rates would cost Scottish households an estimated £1 billion a year in higher mortgage payments.

– Chief Secretary to the Treasury, Danny Alexander

Corporation Tax

The SNP wants to cut the rate of corporation tax – the levy a company pays on its profits – in Scotland to three per cent below the UK level, which currently stands at 21 per cent but is due to fall to 20 per cent next year. It argues that setting Scottish corporation tax at a 'competitive rate' would help boost Scottish economic growth and create as many as 27,000 jobs over the next 20 years. This view is not shared by everyone in the YES campaign. Both the Scottish Greens and RIC have expressed opposition to any corporate tax cut. But the policy remains at the forefront of the SNP's economic strategy.

What the Scottish Government / YES campaign says:

> **London acts as an economic magnet, attracting jobs and investment away from other parts of the UK... [reducing corporation tax] will be one way to secure a competitive advantage and help reverse the loss of corporate headquarters.**
>
> *– Scotland's Future*

What the UK Government / NO campaign says:

> **If Scotland was to go independent, it would be a race to the bottom not just on tax rates, but on wage rates, on terms and conditions, on zero hours contracts, on taking on the energy companies, on reforming the banks. Those who can afford it will be paying less, while hardworking**

families across Scotland will pay more and see their services suffer.
– Leader of the Labour Party, Ed Miliband

Currency Union

The UK's currency is the Pound Sterling. It has traditionally been a high value currency, meaning its relative value is greater than that of many other currencies, including the Euro and the US Dollar. The SNP wants Scotland to continue to use the Pound within a formal currency union after it leaves the UK. Formal currency union would mean Scotland's monetary policy (control over the money supply in the Scottish economy) remained with the Bank of England and the rest of the UK's Treasury in London. It would also require a degree of fiscal co-ordination between an independent Scotland and the rest of the UK, including a limit on Scotland's capacity to borrow and build up debt. In line with the proposals set-out in *Scotland's Future*, the SNP says it will accept these restrictions but argues that currency union would still allow Scotland significant fiscal freedom, including the ability to tailor its tax and spend policies according to its specific needs and preferences. The unionist parties have rejected the SNP's currency proposals, arguing that it would be too risky for the rest of the UK to act as lender of last resort to the Scottish economy. They also claim currency union would mean an effective Westminster veto over Scottish budgets, leaving an independent Scotland with less fiscal autonomy than it has now. The SNP rejects this and has said Scotland will not take a share of the UK's debt without a formal 'sterlingzone' agreement.

What the Scottish Government / YES campaign says:

> The pound is as much Scotland's as it is the rest of the UK's, and the Scottish Government has put forward sensible proposals for a formal monetary union that would ensure both governments had full flexibility over their fiscal policies such as taxation, within an overall sustainable framework.
>
> – *Scottish Government spokesman*

What the UK Government / NO campaign says:

> [Alex Salmond] cannot honestly expect that Scotland would walk away from the rest of the UK, but taxpayers in England, Wales and Northern Ireland would still agree to stand behind the Scottish economy. It is like embarking on a damaging divorce, and insisting we should still share a credit card. In the event that Scotland did vote yes, I would argue just as forcefully against a currency union.
>
> – *Chief Secretary to the Treasury, Danny Alexander*

Debt

In December 2013, the UK's total debt stood at £1.25 trillion, which amounts to 75.5 per cent of the UK's GDP. Some estimates suggest this figure will reach £1.6 trillion, or 86 per cent of GDP, by 2016/17. Were an independent Scotland to accept a population share of the UK's debt (approximately £130 billion), its debt/GDP ratio (including a geographical share of North Sea oil) would be approximately 74 per cent. Were Scotland to accept a 'historical share' of the UK's debt (approximately £85 billion), its debt/GDP ratio could be substantially lower at around 55 per cent. The share of UK debt that an independent

Scotland accepts will be determined by the negotiations that follow a YES vote in the referendum. As mentioned above, the Scottish Government has said an independent Scotland may refuse to accept a share of the UK's debt unless a formal currency union with the rest of the UK is agreed.

What the Scottish Government / YES campaign says:

> The debt belongs legally to the Treasury. [Scotland] can't default on debt that is not legally ours. But we have always said, and I will say again very openly, I that [an independent] Scotland should meet a fair share of the costs of servicing that debt. But assets and liabilities go hand in hand.
> – *Deputy First Minister, Nicola Sturgeon*

What the UK Government / NO campaign says:

> The expectation within the markets is that part of the proper process of independence is taking on a fair share of the debt, and in the end market credibility and confidence is based on the perception that a country is willing to take on its financial obligations.
> – *Chief Secretary to the Treasury, Danny Alexander*

Deficit

Over the year 2012/2013, Scotland ran a net fiscal deficit (the gap between its tax take and expenditure) of 8.3 per cent of GDP. By contrast, the rest of the UK ran net fiscal deficit of 7.3 per cent over the same period. However, for the five years running up to 2012/13, Scotland had smaller current account deficit than the rest of the UK. Forecasts of future Scottish deficits vary. The UK Government claims Scotland will run a deficit of five per cent of GDP in 2016/17, the first year of an

independent Scotland, while the Scottish Government anticipates a 2016/17 deficit of 3.2 per cent. The size of Scotland's
deficit depends to a large extent on the annual flow of North
Sea oil revenues.

What the Scottish Government / YES campaign says:

> The figures show that tax revenues generated in 2012/13
> were £800 higher per head in Scotland compared with
> the UK, meaning that now for every one of the last 33
> years, tax receipts have been higher in Scotland than
> the UK. When looking at the difference between tax
> receipts and spending on everyday services for 2012/13,
> today's report shows Scotland and the UK were both in
> current budget deficit by almost identical amounts as a
> percentage of GDP.
> – First Minister, Alex Salmond

What the UK Government / NO Campaign says:

> The Scottish government's argument for independence
> has been undermined by their own figures. It shows that
> in 2012/13, the Scottish deficit per person was almost
> £500 worse than that of the UK. By 2016/17 this gap is
> forecast to have widened to around £1,000 per person –
> whatever the Scottish government says now, the govern-
> ment of an independent Scotland would be forced to
> raise taxes and cut public services.
> – Chief Secretary to the Treasury, Danny Alexander

Income Tax

Income tax in Scotland is currently set and collected by the UK
Government. People who earn up to £32,000 annually are

taxed at 20 per cent of their income, while people who earn between £32,000 and £150,000 are taxed at 40 per cent of their income. The top rate of the tax in the UK is 45 per cent. This applies to people who earn over £150,000, approximately one per cent of people in Britain. The Labour Party says it will increase the top rate of income tax to 50 per cent if it wins the next UK general election, while the SNP says it has no plans to place Scotland at a 'competitive disadvantage' after independence by reintroducing the 50p top rate. Other parts of the Yes campaign have expressed support for the reintroduction of the 50p top rate. In 2012/13, income tax accounted for 22 per cent of non-North Sea revenue in Scotland.

What the Scottish Government / YES campaign says:

> In terms of the White Paper [on Scottish independence] we said that we don't have proposals for changing taxation, we certainly are not going to put ourselves at a tax disadvantage with the rest of the UK.
> – First Minister, Alex Salmond

What the UK Government / NO campaign says:

> It is an unavoidable fact that Scotland has not run a surplus at any time in the last ten years. To establish a [oil] stablisation fund we would need to cut existing expenditure or raise taxes. That is the price of exposing ourselves to this risk if we vote to leave the UK next year.
> – Better Together chairman, Alistair Darling

Gross Domestic Product (GDP)

GDP is the total market value of everything an economy produces over a specific period of time. A country's GDP is often divided on a per capita (per person) basis. In 2012/13, Scotland's overall GDP was £128 billion excluding North Sea oil revenues and £145 billion including North Sea oil revenues. The first figure puts Scotland's per capita GDP in line with average UK per capita GDP, while the second figure puts it approximately 20 per cent higher. In 2012, the OECD ranked Scotland's per capita GDP (including a geographical share of North Sea oil) as the 14th highest in the world (at $39,642), four places above the UK's (at $35,671).

What the Scottish Government / YES campaign says:

> There is no doubt that Scotland can more than afford to be a successful independent nation. With our vast natural resources, skilled work force and broad-based industrial strengths, Scotland performs strongly against international competitors.
> – SNP Finance Secretary, John Swinney

What the UK Government / NO Campaign says:

> Scotland is already one of the 15 richest economies because it is part of the sixth largest economy in the world, the UK. This success would be put at risk if Scotland became independent. Creating an international border would reduce trade with the rest of the UK. Losing the pound would cost money and jobs as any alternative currency would be worse for the Scottish economy.
> – UK Treasury spokesperson

Oil

Substantial reserves of oil were first discovered in the North Sea in the late 1960s and production began in 1975. North Sea tax revenues steadily increased up until the mid-1980s, peaking in 1984/85 at £12 billion (£25 billion at 2009/10 prices). Since then revenues have varied, from a low of two to three billion per year in the early 1990s, to another peak of £12.9 billion in 2008/09. Experts disagree over the extent of future revenues. The Office for Budget Responsibility (OBR) expects oil tax returns to be as low as £3.3 billion in 2016/17, while the Scottish Government anticipates revenues of between £6.8 billion and £7.9 billion for the same year. Although North Sea reserves have been declining since 1999, most analysts expect production of some sort to continue until the mid-21st century. A median line division of North Sea territory would give an independent Scotland control over 90 per cent remaining oil reserves.

What the Scottish Government / YES campaign says:

> **Successive Westminster Governments have failed to provide effective stewardship of Scotland's oil and gas resources... For the sake of future generations living and bringing up their families in Scotland, we must not lose out on the opportunity that remaining reserves provide.**
> *– Scotland's Future*

What the UK Government / NO campaign says:

> **What we see with the North Sea is a great success story for the United Kingdom – and now the oil and gas is getting harder to recover it is more important than ever that the North Sea oil and gas industry has the backing of the whole of the United Kingdom.**
> *– Prime Minister, David Cameron*

Sterlingisation

If no formal currency union can be agreed, the Scottish Government may decide to continue to use the Pound unilaterally. This would be called 'Sterlingisation'. Under these conditions, Scotland would keep the Pound as its currency but without the consent of the rest of the UK. The Bank of England would continue to set Scotland's monetary policy but it would not act as lender of last resort to the Scottish economy.

What the Scottish Government / YES Campaign says:

> It is a simple fact that sterling is an internationally tradeable currency – the pound is as much Scotland's as the rest of the UK's and there is nothing that George Osborne or anyone else can do to stop us using it.
> – *First Minister, Alex Salmond*

What the UK Government / NO Campaign says:

> [Sterlingisation] would mean Scotland's interest rates would be set by what would then be a foreign country. Worse than that, a separate Scotland would have to make substantial cuts in public spending. [Sterlingisation] would cost jobs and put up the cost of mortgages.
> – *Better Together chairman, Alistair Darling*

Separate Currency

An independent Scotland may decide to abandon the Pound altogether and establish a separate Scottish currency. This would mean that Scottish monetary policy was set by a Scottish Central Bank (SCB), leaving the Scottish Government free to design a monetary and exchange rate regime suited to Scotland's specific economic needs. Supporters of this policy, such as the

7

Scottish Greens, argue that it would give Scotland full control over its macroeconomic strategy. Opponents claim it would create monetary instability and disrupt cross-border trade.

What the Scottish Government / YES Campaign says:

YES

It would cost the rest of the UK, particularly English businesses, £500 million if George Osborne succeeded in shoving Scotland out of Sterling. I don't think that's a credible thing for a Chancellor to say... Our position is that we should share a currency and therefore there is no transaction costs.
– *First Minister, Alex Salmond*

What the UK Government / NO Campaign says:

NO

Launching a new currency now in arguably the most turbulent economic times we have seen in modern times. You would be asking people to take a gamble on a currency that is wide open to manipulation and open to speculation as oil prices rise and fall. It is an absolutely ridiculous policy that would be gambling with Scotland's future.
– *Better Together chairman, Alistair Darling*

The Issues: Welfares and Pensions

8

State Pensions

The Basic State Pension is part of the United Kingdom's pension arrangements alongside the Graduated Retirement Benefit and State Earnings-Related Pension Scheme (or SERPS, now known as the State Second Pension). The State Pension is a 'contribution-based' benefit and depends on an individual's history of National Insurance (NI) contributions – for those with 30 years' payments a flat rate of £113.10 is paid per week (as of 2014–15), but a smaller pro-rata rate for someone with fewer qualifying years.

The State Pension Age (SPA) is currently 65 for men and will eventually be the same for women, although it is in the process of being increased from 60. However, the 2011 Pensions Act will raise the SPA to 66 for both men and women by 6 October 2010, while under the earlier 2007 Pensions Act it will be raised to 67 for everyone between 2034and 2036, and to 68 between 2044–46. The Scottish Government plans to reconsider the SPA if Scotland becomes independent, while also increasing the State Pension using a 'triple lock' from 2016 so that payments increase by average earnings, inflation or 2.5 per cent, whichever is highest. Unionists argue that with Scotland's population ageing faster than the rest of the UK then funding such proposals would be unaffordable.

There is also a lot of debate about what Better Together calls a 'demographic time-bomb', in other words the fact that – in future – Scotland will have a bigger proportion of people of retirement age and fewer people working than in other parts of the UK, something the Scottish Government disputes. Unionists say the best way of defusing this 'time-bomb' is by sharing 'the burden across 60 million people, not just the five

8

million who live in Scotland', while those who support independence argue that as the proportion of tax revenues taken up by spending on social protection (including State Pensions) is presently lower in Scotland than the UK, then 'these benefits are currently more affordable here' and would remain so under independence.

In June 2014 the Scottish Government's Expert Working Group on Welfare published its second report aimed at ensuring a Scottish welfare system that was 'fair, personal and simple'. Its 40 recommendations included re-establishing the link between benefits and the cost of living, increasing the Carer's Allowance by £575 a year and abolishing the Work Capability Assessment, all measures Nicola Sturgeon pledged would be introduced in the event of independence. The Scottish Labour Party, meanwhile, criticised it as 'the most cynical type of politics', everyone being 'offered more money, or less taxation, with no means of explaining how any of it is paid for'.

What the Scottish Government / YES campaign says:

> **We will ensure that current pensioners will receive their pensions as now, on time and in full. All accrued rights will be honoured and protected, and planned reforms will be rolled out, including the single-tier pension.**
> *– Scotland's Future*

What the UK Government / NO campaign says:

> **The UK State Pension means that everybody right across the UK gets equal access to a pension regardless of where in the UK you were born, have lived or worked... By spreading the responsibility across the broader**

shoulders of the UK it is easier for us to support all of
our pensioners equally in good times and bad.
– bettertogether.net

Private and public service pensions

As well as the UK Government-administered State Pension,
many Scots also have schemes accrued in the private or public
sector and at present these are protected (for example in the
event of a company going bust) by the UK Pensions Protection
Fund. Better Together warns that there exists 'no credible plans
to replicate this in an independent Scotland', although the
Scottish Government says they would remain 'fully protected'.
There is also an on-going debate about the impact of European
Union rules that mean pension schemes administered in more
than one Member State have to be 'fully funded'.

What the Scottish Government / YES campaign says:

> This Scottish Government supports the continued roll-
> out of automatic enrolment, introduced last year, to help
> address the historic decline in private pension saving.
> With independence, we would establish a Scottish Employ-
> ment Savings Trust to provide a workplace pension
> scheme focused on people with low to moderate earn-
> ings, which will accept any employer wishing to use it. In
> an independent Scotland, all public service pension rights
> and entitlements will be fully protected and accessible.
> – *Scotland's Future*

What the UK Government / NO campaign says:

> Going it alone would... bring with it a major challenge to
> our private pension schemes. Under EU rules, if a pension

YES

8

NO

scheme is run in more than one member state then it needs to immediately be fully funded. Many of the private schemes that Scots are members of fall into this category and would, as a result of independence, face financial problems so severe that it could force many of them to close.
– *bettertogether.net*

Welfare

The Welfare State consists of public spending by the UK government on a range of services intended to improve health, employment and social security. At present it is administered on a UK-wide basis with claimants receiving the same level of benefit payments (for example Jobseekers' Allowance) regardless of where they live in Scotland, England and Wales (the Northern Irish Assembly has some discretion over how payments are made, but not the amount). Although the Scottish Parliament/Government controls some minor aspects of the Welfare State (for example Council Tax benefit), policy and delivery is largely the responsibility of Westminster.

Recent changes to the Welfare State include the introduction of an 'under-occupancy' charge (dubbed the 'bedroom tax' by critics) for those living in social housing, as well as the roll out of a new Universal Credit and Personal Independent Payments (PIPs) which combine several existing benefits into one. The Conservative-Liberal Democrat UK Coalition says this will simplify social security payments while saving the taxpayer money and ensuring that those reliant on benefits do not lose out financially if they find work. The SNP Scottish Government, however, says it wants to abolish the 'bedroom tax' and, if there is a YES vote, would halt the further roll out of the Universal Credit and PIPs in Scotland.

What the Scottish Government / YES campaign says:

YES✗

> The current Westminster Government's approach to welfare has consistently been rejected by a majority of Scottish MPs and MSPs. If we leave welfare in Westminster's hands, our welfare state is likely to be changed beyond recognition. Universal Credit and Personal Independence Payments have suffered from controversy and delay, and have created significant anxiety amongst some of our most vulnerable people. The unfairness of the 'bedroom tax' is well known. We believe it is possible to design an efficient and fair welfare system that meets the needs of those who depend on it, and treats them with dignity and respect while supporting those who can to find work.
> – *Scotland's Future*

What the UK Government / NO campaign says:

✗NO

> The UK welfare system is based on need not nationality. It means we can support people equally right across the UK. Pooling and sharing our resources across the UK makes higher benefit spending in Scotland more affordable. Without a serious plan for welfare or details of how it would be funded, the nationalists' uncosted welfare promises are simply not credible. The creation of the welfare state is one of our nations' greatest achievements. Through working together we have established a system which puts solidarity into action to support those in our

society in the greatest need. It means that if you are out of work in Glasgow your benefits are paid by the taxes of someone working in Glamorgan. Similarly, when you retire in Lanark your pension is paid by the taxes of a young person in Liverpool starting out in working life.
– *bettertogether.net*

Health

The National Health Service (NHS) is almost 70 years old and has been administered separately in Scotland since its inception – under the National Health Service (Scotland) Act 1947 – although at the same time it is part of a UK-wide health service, free at the point of use. However in some respects health policy has followed different paths in Scotland and England since the NHS came under control of the Scottish Parliament in 1999. The former prefers to keep private sector involvement to a minimum, while Labour and Conservative governments at Westminster have pursued a more free-market approach to delivering healthcare (although still without charge to users).

What the Scottish Government / YES campaign says:

Scotland faces long-standing challenges in health outcomes which are strongly associated with economic and social disadvantage. With independence, Scotland can work towards a fairer society that will address these health inequalities. Independence will not affect the day-to-day management of the NHS in Scotland, nor how people access NHS services. Similarly, it will not mean ending current cross-border arrangements with

8

health services in the rest of the UK, which have continued even though the NHS in Scotland already operates independently.
– *Scotland's Future*

What the UK Government / NO campaign says:

One of the great things about the UK is that if you or your family need specialist treatment you can get it anywhere in the UK, free of charge on the NHS. When Sally [Russell, a Better Together volunteer] needed a double lung transplant she benefited from brilliant NHS care, across the UK. The Freeman Hospital [in Newcastle], where Sally was treated, is one of the best places in the world for the specialist care she needed. Today you get any treatment you or your family needs, for free, at any NHS hospital in the UK. Why risk more complication and cost when you can get the specialist care you need now?
– *bettertogether.net*

8

The Issues: Defence and Foreign Affairs

European Union (EU)

As explained in Chapter 2, the EU is a partnership of 28 Member States of which Scotland (as part of the UK) has been a member since 1973. It is based on a series of international treaties, signed and approved by all EU Member States, the most recent being the Lisbon Treaty that came into force in December 2009. Speaking in Bruges in April, Alex Salmond said Scotland was a 'lynchpin of Europe's future' and would, as a successor state to the UK, inherit its membership of the EU once it becomes independent. The SNP argues that the conditions of Scotland's independent EU membership will be negotiated within 18 months of the independence referendum.

The UK government and Better Together, however, warn that EU membership would not be as quick or straightforward as the Scottish Government claims. They point out that the accession of an independent Scotland would require the assent of every existing Member State and that an objection from, for example, Spain (in which Catalonia is pushing for a similar referendum on secession) might see Scotland ejected. Even if it were admitted, argue unionists, Scotland might be compelled to join the Euro and Schengen passport-free area (both usual conditions for new EU countries), while it might struggle to retain a share of the UK's EU budget rebate.

Formally, the European Commission has stated that, as an independent Scotland would be a 'third country' (ie not an existing Member State), it would need to apply for membership. José Manuel Barroso, the current Commission President, has also rejected the idea that an independent Scotland could negotiate membership of the EU while still part of the UK (ie between the referendum in September 2014 and 'independence

9

day' in March 2016). Several respected experts in European law and politics, however, dispute this position, as does the Scottish Government, which points to Greenland (which left the EU despite being part of Denmark) and East Germany (which joined as part of Germany following reunification) as examples of the EU's flexibility. At the May 2014 European elections, the SNP received 29 per cent of the vote and two MEPs, Labour 25 per cent of the vote and two MEPs, the Conservatives 12 per cent of the vote and one MEP and UKIP 10 per cent of the vote and one MEP. UKIP won the European election across the rest of the UK, taking 30 per cent of the vote and 23 MEPs.

What the Scottish Government / YES campaign says:

YES

> Scotland's vast natural resources and human talent make it one of the lynchpins of the European Union. Our huge energy reserves, our economic and financial contribution, our fishing grounds, our academic, cultural and social links, and our commitment to the founding values of the European ideal place us at the very heart of the EU.
> – *First Minister, Alex Salmond*

What the UK Government / NO campaign says:

NO

> Scotland's negotiations to join the EU are likely to be complex and long and the outcome would certainly prove less advantageous than the status quo. People in Scotland deserve to have the available facts ahead of making one of the most important political decisions in the history of our union. The terms of EU membership which your government has said it will seek to secure

for an independent Scotland are at odds with the EU's own rules of membership.
– *UK Foreign Secretary, William Hague*

North Atlantic Treaty Organisation (NATO)

NATO is a western military alliance. It was founded in 1949 to act as a bulwark against Soviet power. It currently has 28 members, including the United States, France and Germany and a number of small northern European countries, such as Norway and Denmark. As part of the UK, Scotland is also a member. The SNP has a long history of opposition to Scottish membership of NATO, principally because of NATO's commitment to nuclear weapons. But it reversed that opposition at its October 2012 conference. The policy shift was opposed by many inside and outside the party, who argued that membership of NATO would compromise an independent Scotland's ability to remove British nuclear weapons from Scottish waters. This view is echoed by many opponents of independence who argue that NATO will refuse Scotland's membership application if Britain's Trident nuclear weapons system is forced from its current base on the Clyde. The SNP, however, insists Scotland can be a non-nuclear member of the Alliance, in line with 25 of the 28 current member states. The question of independent Scottish membership of NATO may have been complicated by US President Barack Obama's stated support for a 'strong and united' United Kingdom.

What the Scottish Government / YES campaign says:

> Scotland is in a vital geo-strategic position with the Iceland Gap to our north, the Atlantic to our west and

the North Sea to our East. The SNP has committed itself to security stability with our neighbouring northern allies who are all NATO members. With a commitment to conventional maritime priorities we will be a reliable and dependable partner.
– SNP defence spokesman, Angus Robertson

What the UK Government / NO campaign says:

NATO, as an alliance with nuclear deterrence as a central part of its strategic concept, could hardly be expected to welcome a new member state whose government put in jeopardy the continued operation of the UK independent nuclear deterrent – a deterrent which protects not only the UK but all of Nato as well.
– UK Secretary of Defence, Philip Hammond

Scottish Defence Force

The SNP plans to create an independent Scottish Defence Force (SDF) of 15,000 regular and 5,000 reserve personnel. The SDF would be funded by a military budget reduced from the £3 billion Scotland currently spends as part of the UK to £2.5 billion, bringing Scottish defence expenditure down to around 1.7 per cent of GDP, roughly into line with the Nordic average. (Norway spends 1.6 per cent of its GDP on defence, while Denmark and Finland each spend 1.5 per cent and Sweden spends 1.3 per cent.) The SNP's defence plans designate Faslane, currently the home of the UK's submarine-based nuclear deterrent, as the base of a future Scottish navy. This navy would include two frigates and up to six patrol boats from the Royal Navy's current fleet. The SDF would also include a tactical air support squadron. Other parts of the Yes campaign, such as the Scottish Greens and RIC, envisage a much smaller independent Scottish defence structure.

What the Scottish Government / YES campaign says:

YES

An independent Scotland will have first-class conventional forces playing a full role in defending the country as well as cooperating with international partners and neighbours.

– SNP Minister for Transport and Veterans, Keith Brown

What the UK Government / NO campaign says:

NO

The UK armed forces are a highly integrated and very sophisticated fighting force. The idea that you can sort of break off a little bit, like a square on a chocolate bar and that would be the bit that went north of the Border, is frankly laughable.

– UK Secretary of Defence, Philip Hammond

UK Defence

The UK's defence budget is currently £34 billion – the fourth largest, in real terms, of any country in the world after the United States, China and Russia. There are around 100,000 troops in the British army, but this number is due to fall to around 80,000 by 2018. Britain's Royal Air Force has 35,000 regular and 1,500 auxiliary personnel, as well as more than 100 BAE System Hawk aircraft. The Royal Navy has approximately 36,000 personnel, both regular and reserve. A review of Britain's defence force in 2010 led to a series of cuts in UK defence expenditure. This included the aforementioned reduction in troop numbers and an amalgamation of historic Scottish regiments into larger regiments.

What the Scottish Government / YES campaign says:

YES

Scotland has suffered hugely disproportionate personnel cuts and the MoD should be transparent about their latest round of redundancies. With personnel levels at an all-time low in Scotland the time has come to make better defence decisions closer to home. Scotland requires 15,000 regular personnel which can and will be delivered with independence.
– SNP defence spokesman, Angus Robertson

What the UK Government / NO campaign says:

NO

As part of the UK, Scotland benefits from the full range of UK defence capabilities and activities. These defend UK airspace, patrol the surrounding seas and help to protect everyone in the UK against both natural and man-made threats.
– UK Government Defence Analysis Report

Trident

Trident is the UK's submarine-based nuclear deterrent. It is stationed at two bases on the west coast of Scotland, Faslane and Coulport. It was acquired in the 1980s as a replacement for the Polaris missile system. Trident is made-up of four submarines carrying a total of 16 missiles and three warheads. The current generation of submarines will reach the end their working lives over the next ten to 15 years. The Conservatives and the Labour Party are committed to a like-for-like replacement of Trident, while the Liberal Democrats favour a scaled-down missile system. The SNP, along with the Scottish Greens, the SSP and RIC, want to scrap Trident altogether. The UK Government says it would cost between £15 billion and £20

9

billion to replace Trident, while the Scottish Campaign for Nuclear Disarmament (SCND) estimates the total cost, including long-term maintenance, at closer to £90 billion. Estimates vary as to the number of jobs that depend on Trident's presence at Faslane and Coulport. Labour has suggested the figure might be as high as 19,000, including indirect employment in local businesses. However, a Freedom of Information request by SCND to the Ministry of Defence revealed the number could as low as 670. The final decision on whether or not to renew Trident will be made in 2016. Following a YES vote, the SNP says it intends to remove Trident from Scottish waters by the end of the first term of an independent parliament, or in the 'fastest and safest time possible'.

What the Scottish Government / YES campaign says:

Westminster is determined to retain the UK's nuclear arsenal, squandering billions of pounds on something that most Scots believe is neither wanted nor needed. Only a YES vote for an independent Scotland can rid Scotland of nuclear weapons.
– YES Scotland chief executive, Blair Jenkins

What the UK Government / NO campaign says:

While there continues to be significant risks of further proliferation and other states retain much larger nuclear weapons arsenals, successive governments have been clear the UK will retain a minimum credible deterrent as the ultimate guarantee of our security.
– Foreign Office Minister, Baroness Warsi

Shipbuilding

At the beginning of the 20th century up to one fifth of the world's ship were built on the River Clyde. Since then the shipbuilding industry in Scotland has steadily declined. Today, Scottish shipyards account for a much smaller proportion of global output. Roughly 3,200 people are employed by BAE Systems in Govan, Scotstoun, Filton and Rosyth. However, BAE is due to shed 835 of these jobs between 2014 and 2016. In 2013 a row broke-out after the UK Government decided to award contracts to build new Type 26 Destroyers to the Govan and Scotstoun yards instead of the Portsmouth yard. This fuelled the debate over the future of shipbuilding in an independent Scotland. Unionists argue that Royal Navy contracts will no longer go to Scottish yards if Scotland leaves the UK, while nationalists insist Scottish shipyard workers have the skills and expertise to compete for and win contracts in the global market place.

What the Scottish Government / YES campaign says:

> There is nothing to prevent ships for the rest of the UK being built in an independent Scotland... An independent Scotland will have its own requirements for Type 26 ships and offshore patrol vessels. What a Yes vote also offers is an opportunity for a government with full economic powers to develop a shipbuilding strategy specifically for Scotland, in partnership with industry and workforce.
> – *Deputy First Minister, Nicola Sturgeon*

What the UK Government / NO campaign says:

> The defence industry employs thousands of people in Scotland because we are part of the UK. If we walk away

9

from the UK then we walk away from the UK investment that sustains the jobs of so many communities throughout Scotland. The UK government has never built a warship outside of the UK. The idea that we could leave the UK but UK warships would continue to be built here simply isn't credible.

– Better Together spokesperson

UN Security Council

Established in 1946 in the wake of the Second World War, the United Nations Security Council (UNSC) is the primary body of the United Nations. It is charged with responsibility for the 'maintenance of international peace and security'. The UNSC has five permanent and ten revolving members. The five permanent members are the United States, France, China, Russia and the UK. Supporters of the Union contend that the UK's permanent UNSC seat provides Scotland with an influence in international affairs it would lack were to it become an independent country. They also argue that Scotland's departure from the UK – and the abolition of the Trident nuclear system that may result from it – would lead to Britain's expulsion from the UNSC. Pointing to the fact that Russia inherited the USSR's place on the Security Council after the break-up of the Soviet Union, the SNP says Scottish independence will have no bearing on the UK's UNSC seat.

What the Scottish Government / YES campaign says:

As the achievements of other countries show influence is not about size, it's about working together and how you use the powers that you have... 50 countries have become independent since 1945 and countries around

the world more than understand the principle of being responsible for your own decisions.
– SNP defence spokesman, Angus Robertson

What the UK Government / NO campaign says:

NO

The UK's aim and claim to continue to play a major role in world affairs would be undermined by Scottish separation, because even a debate about whether the UK should continue to be a member of the UN Security Council, for example, would do damage to its reputation.
– House of Lords Committee on Soft Power

Embassies

The YES campaign envisions an independent Scotland having a network of between 70 and 90 overseas embassies. These will be 'based on existing Scottish international offices and [Scotland's] share of UK overseas assets' and will be charged with promoting Scottish trade and other international economic opportunities. Nationalists say that the budget for Scotland's overseas network will be 'significantly lower' than the contribution Scottish taxpayers currently make to the running costs of the UK's embassy network. In January 2013, Foreign Office minister David Lidington warned that an independent Scotland would not be able to match the scale of Britain's embassy network, which has 270 offices worldwide and 14,000 staff.

What the YES campaign / Scottish Government says:

YES

Already, Scotland, as a devolved country, has 22 offices across the world. Clearly, as an independent country, we would build that presence. The [Foreign and Commonwealth Office] has a very large network of embassies

around the world, to some extent – not entirely – but to some extent a legacy of empire, that is focused not just on trade, but on military objectives as well. It would certainly be the objective of an independent Scottish government to replicate the quality of the representation that is provided, not necessarily doing it in exactly the same way with exactly the same property footprint.
– *Deputy First Minister, Nicola Sturgeon*

What the NO campaign / UK Government says:

An independent Scotland would not replicate that sort of network. We need to know what sort of network they envisage. I'm very far from clear how an independent Scotland would provide the diplomatic network and have to protect the Scotch Whisky Association, Scottish financial services and the defence companies from Scotland, particularly given their positions on defence.
– *Foreign Office minister, David Lidington*

The Issues: Culture and
Identity

10

Social Union

How Scotland might relate to the rest of the United Kingdom after independence is a central issue in the referendum debate. The SNP says Scots will continue to share a 'social union' with people in England, Wales and Northern Ireland. The social union will be based on the common cultural, familial and institutional ties that Scots, English, Welsh and Northern Irish people have developed over centuries of political cooperation. In line with the proposals set out in Scotland's Future, one of these common institutional ties will be the current British monarchy, which the SNP wants to retain in an independent Scotland. However, this position is opposed by many activists in broader the YES campaign who favour an independent Scottish republic.

What the YES campaign / Scottish Government says:

> What remains unchanged [after independence] is that which matters to people across these islands; our social union, which we share and works well. From the monarchy and the BBC and other common institutions, much will continue as today.
> – *Angus Robertson*

What the NO campaign / UK Government says:

> The UK is more than an economic and political union. It is also a social union, enabling us to work together across the four nations of the UK for the benefit of us all. It is this social union which allows us to tackle social injustice and inequality wherever it exists in the UK.
> – *Alistair Darling*

10

Identity

Identity is also a central issue in the referendum debate. Research suggests that the more strongly Scottish a voter feels, the more likely he or she is support independence, while the more strongly British a voter feels, the more likely he or she is to vote against independence. The YES campaign insists that a strong sense of Britishness is not a barrier to support for independence, but the No campaign claims many Scots feel the referendum is forcing them to choose between their Scottish and British identities. In April, an ICM poll found that, while there was a majority for independence among Scots born in Scotland, English-born Scots were much more hostile to the prospect of Scotland's departure from the UK. Separate studies have indicated disproportionately high levels of support for independence among other national identities and ethnic groups in Scotland, such as Polish-Scots and Asian-Scots.

What the YES campaign / Scottish Government says:

> **Britishness will exist in Scotland long after we become independent. In fact I think it could well be enhanced with independence. With independence we will get opportunity to define a new Britishness, one based on equality and mutual respect.**
> – *SNP MP, Pete Wishart*

What the NO campaign / UK Government says:

> **[Scottish separatism] insists that identification with one of our nations is diminished by identification with our country as a whole. After all, [the SNP] want to force people to choose to be Scottish or British. I say you can be both.**
> – *Ed Miliband*

10

Immigration

Over recent decades, immigration to Scotland has been disproportionately lower than it has been to many other parts of the UK, notably London and the English south east. The YES campaign believes independence would help redress that imbalance by allowing Scotland to develop a more liberal immigration system. *Scotland's Future* sets out plans to increase the number of immigrants, particularly young, skilled workers, to Scotland by creating a points-based immigration system for non-EU applicants. The YES campaign has also said an independent Scotland would relax rules regarding asylum seekers and refugees, including by abandoning the practice of 'dawn raids' and abolishing Gartnavel detention centre. By contrast, Labour and the Conservatives (although not the Liberal Democrats) have both promised to tighten the UK immigration system.

What the YES campaign / Scottish Government says:

> Scotland has an immigration policy imposed on it by Westminster that simply isn't working for Scotland. [We] need the powers of independence to develop an immigration that works for Scotland.
> – *SNP MSP, Derek McKay*

What the NO campaign / UK Government says:

> Immigration policy has consequences for border controls of course but we simply don't know what the SNP immigration policy would be. What we do know is that scale of additional migration needed can't simply be made-up by university graduates.
> – *Yvette Cooper*

10

Citizenship

According to *Scotland's Future*, the initial automatic criteria for citizenship of an independent Scotland will be habitual residence (those who are resident in Scotland) and birth (those who were born in Scotland). After independence, other people will be able to apply for Scottish citizenship, including people with a Scottish parent or grandparent and those with a 'demonstrable connection' to Scotland (such as having lived in Scotland for a period of ten years or so). Although the SNP favours a system of post-independence dual Scottish-UK citizenship for any Scot who would like it, the UK Home Secretary Theresa May has indicated such an agreement could be rejected by the rest of the UK.

What the YES campaign / Scottish Government say:

> Already, Scotland, as a devolved country, has 22 offices across the world. Clearly, as an independent country, we would build that presence. The [Foreign and Commonwealth Office] has a very large network of embassies around the world, to some extent – not entirely – but to some extent a legacy of empire, that is focused not just on trade, but on military objectives as well. It would certainly be the objective of an independent Scottish government to replicate the quality of the representation that is provided, not necessarily doing it in exactly the same way with exactly the same property footprint.
> – *Deputy First Minister, Nicola Sturgeon*

What the NO campaign / UK Governmnent say:

> An independent Scotland would not replicate that sort of network. We need to know what sort of network they

10

NO envisage. I'm very far from clear how an independent Scotland would provide the diplomatic network and have to protect the Scotch Whisky Association, Scottish financial services and the defence companies from Scotland, particularly given their positions on defence.
– Foreign Office minister, David Lidington

Broadcasting

After independence, the SNP intends to create a new Scottish Broadcasting Service (SBS) to replace the BBC. As well as producing more Scottish-based content, the SBS will purchase and continue to broadcast popular BBC shows such as *Eastenders* and *Match of the Day*. However, some have suggested that viewers in an independent Scotland may be charged for access to specific BBC services, such as its online content, while Scottish Conservative leader Ruth Davidson has warned that the SNP 'simply cannot guarantee [Scotland] would still get Doctor Who after independence'.

What the YES campaign / Scottish Government says:

[Independence] means we can move forward with a clear ambition to deliver a new approach to broadcasting which will increase production opportunities in Scotland through a new Scottish Broadcasting Service; new powers over the economy to encourage our culture and creative sectors; and increased opportunities to build our international reputation for culture, heritage and creativity.
– Scotland's Future

What the NO campaign / UK Governmnent says:

Alex Salmond has told us he's going to break up the BBC with no details about how he would do it or what it means for Scottish independence or people whose jobs rely on out TV industry.
– Labour MP, Margaret Curran

NO

10

What Happens after YES?

The exact political consequences of a YES vote on September 18 are difficult to predict. If the YES campaign's margin of victory is slight (less than three or four per cent, for instance) some supporters of the Union may claim the SNP lacks a clear 'moral' mandate to pursue independence. But these claims are unlikely to change the outcome of the referendum, particularly if the vote is judged by official observers to have been conducted in line with international standards of fairness and transparency. Once the YES vote has been formally recognised by the UK Government, the Scottish Government will begin negotiations to take Scotland out of the UK. These negotiations will cover a range of issues – such as the possibility of a currency union between Scotland and the rest of the UK, the removal of Trident from Scottish waters and Scotland's membership of the EU – and be conducted in conjunction with a range of organisations, including the EU and NATO. The Scottish Government believes negotiations can be concluded within 18 months of a YES vote in September, in time for Scotland's formal departure from the UK in March 2016, although the NO campaign disputes this timeline. In May 2016, Scots will go to the polls to elect their first democratic independent Parliament. The precise composition of that Parliament won't be known until after the election. But it is likely to include a substantial contingent from Scotland's two largest political parties, the SNP and Labour, alongside representatives from smaller parties, such the Scottish Conservatives and the Scottish Greens. New parties may emerge in the aftermath of a YES vote. Once the shape of the Parliament has been become clear, the process of drawing up a new independent Scottish constitution will begin. In the event of a YES vote, the Scottish Government intends to invite Scottish politicians from unionist parties to help negotiate the terms of independence. 'Team Scotland' could include Labour's shadow Defence Secretary Douglas Alexander and current Secretary of State for Scotland Alistair Carmichael. However, a number of journalists, artists and campaigners recently called for the creation of a 'citizens' assembly' to stop politicians 'carving Scotland up' after the referendum. The 2015 UK general election could be a complicating factor in the independence negotiations, particularly if the Labour Party secures a substantial number of seats in Scotland but fails to win a commanding or outright majority in the House of Commons. If this is the case, calls from within the Labour Party for Scotland to remain part of the UK are likely to increase. In June, the SNP published its proposed interim constitution for an independent Scotland. It included a constitutional prohibition on the stationing of nuclear weapons in Scottish waters, enshrining the right of each Scottish citizen to a home and an education, an retaining the current monarch as head of state. The SNP said it would be replaced by a permanent constitution after Scotland became fully independent in 2016.

YES Vote Timeline

- **Autumn/Winter 2014 – Following a YES vote, independence negotiations begin**
- **5 May 2015 – The last scheduled UK General Election in which Scots can participate takes place**
- **24 March 2016 – The Act of Union is formally dissolved and Scotland becomes an independent country**
- **5 May 2016 – Elections to an independent Scottish Parliament take place and Scots elect their first democratic independent government**

11

What Happens after YES?

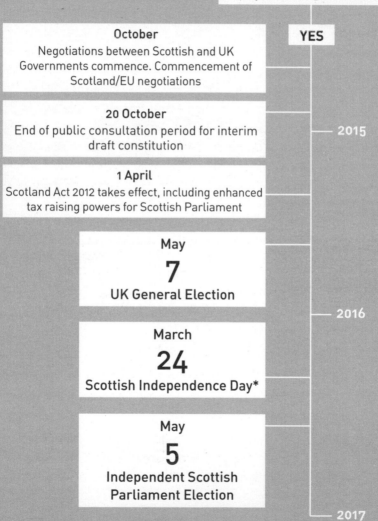

September **18** Independence Referendum

YES

October
Negotiations between Scottish and UK Governments commence. Commencement of Scotland/EU negotiations

20 October
End of public consultation period for interim draft constitution

— 2015

1 April
Scotland Act 2012 takes effect, including enhanced tax raising powers for Scottish Parliament

May 7 UK General Election

— 2016

March 24 Scottish Independence Day*

May 5 Independent Scottish Parliament Election

— 2017

* MPs for Scottish Constituencies (59) cease to be MPs – which may result in a change in UK Government

What Happens after NO?

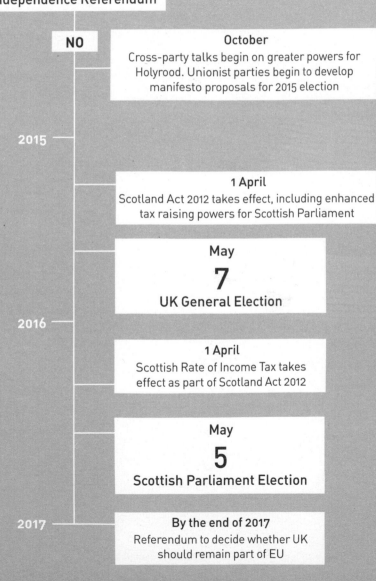

September
18
Independence Referendum

NO

October
Cross-party talks begin on greater powers for Holyrood. Unionist parties begin to develop manifesto proposals for 2015 election

2015

1 April
Scotland Act 2012 takes effect, including enhanced tax raising powers for Scottish Parliament

May
7
UK General Election

2016

1 April
Scottish Rate of Income Tax takes effect as part of Scotland Act 2012

May
5
Scottish Parliament Election

2017

By the end of 2017
Referendum to decide whether UK should remain part of EU

What Happens after NO?

As with a YES vote, it is difficult to say with complete certainty what will happen if a majority of Scots vote NO on 18 September 2014. A lot will depend on the margin of victory. For example if independence is defeated by a heavy margin then the UK government and other Unionist parties will probably feel under less pressure than if, say, the NO vote wins by less than one per cent, as was the case in a similar referendum on Quebec 'sovereignty' (or independence from Canada) in 1995.

It seems likely, however, that the three Unionist parties – Labour, Conservative and Liberal Democrat – will move quickly to demonstrate that their joint declaration of 'more powers' made on 16 June at Edinburgh's Calton Hill was sincere. Although there is a degree of overlap between the parties' proposals, they would have to meet in some forum or other to negotiate the details. Once this reaches a conclusion then each party has promised to include proposals for further devolution in their respective manifestos for both the 2015 UK general election and 2016 Scottish Parliament contest.

In March 2013 Douglas Alexander, a Scottish Labour MP and his party's Shadow Foreign Secretary, proposed that a 'National Convention' might meet to reach agreement, not just on the powers of the Scottish Parliament but also common goals for the future of Scotland. What he called 'Scotland 2025' would include not only politicians but also members of civic society to consider the country's economic, social and cultural priorities over the next decade or so.

Speaking at Edinburgh University, Alexander said a National Convention (modelled on the old Scottish Constitutional Convention) could 'create a space for a new kind of politics'. He added:

12

It could help change the way power is distributed and shared. And it could genuinely help put people in charge of writing the next chapter of Scotland's story. It could make sure that the debate that the next 19 months will bring is not lost. And rather than pretending politicians have all the answers, it could engage the people of Scotland in deliberating together a new vision for an old nation.

Perhaps significantly, both the Liberal Democrats and Conservatives have made positive noises about Alexander's proposal, suggesting it is the most likely outcome in the event of a NO vote.

In another speech, also in March 2013, the Scottish Conservative leader Ruth Davidson also spoke of finding (assuming a NO vote) 'a means whereby we do not lurch from one commission to another, year after year; where the constitutional and commercial certainty we all crave is never reached'. 'Where devolution is not viewed as a bilateral arrangement between Holyrood and Westminster, Cardiff Bay and Westminster or Stormont and Westminster,' she added, 'but a mechanism which reviews devolution across – and within – our whole United Kingdom.'

This hinted at a more formal reorganisation of the UK's constitutional machinery, and given Davidson's speech was delivered with the approval of Downing Street then it is probably a fair guide to the UK government's intentions post-September 2014. The Scottish Liberal Democrats, meanwhile, want to go much further if independence is rejected in the referendum. In early 2014 Sir Menzies Campbell, a former UK Lib Dem leader who also presided over the party's plans for a federal UK, set out a 'timetable for action' following a NO vote.

Sir Menzies argued that the Calman Commission process (under which the three Unionist parties agreed more powers for Holyrood, later enacted in the 2012 Scotland Act) was 'a persuasive example of what can be achieved' if parties worked closely together. He then set out the following process:

- **Provisions in the 2015 Queen's Speech to 'strengthen the powers of Scotland within the United Kingdom'.**

- **Led by the Scotland Office, the UK Government should analyse the options available to enhance the powers of the Scottish Parliament.**

- **The Scottish Government should share officials' 'research and knowledge' to inform this process.**

- **The Scottish Parliament should ensure the independent fiscal body which will support the tax powers in the 2012 Scotland Act is designed to cope with other financial powers should they be devolved following a NO vote.**

- **The Secretary of State for Scotland should convene a meeting within 30 days of the referendum to 'secure a consensus for the further extension of powers to the Scottish Parliament consistent with continued membership of the United Kingdom and to be included in party manifestos for the 2015 general election'.**

- **Political parties should include commitments in their May 2015 election manifestos.**

- **The necessary changes should be made through a further Scotland Act, which would also see the 'entrench-**

ment' of (ie making permanent) the Scottish Parliament via resolutions at Westminster and Holyrood.

Sir Menzies also argued there was a consensus – based on contributions from politicians, think tanks, civic organisations and academics – around two propositions. First, the Scottish Parliament should raise the majority of its own spending via improved tax powers. And second (as mentioned above), Holyrood should be permanently entrenched or, to use Gordon Brown's preferred word, made 'indissoluble'.

Both propositions, observed Sir Menzies, were 'entirely normal in federal systems around the world', and indeed that remains the Liberal Democrats' preferred destination should a majority of Scots vote NO in September 2014 – a UK federation with a written constitution and formal division of powers between the federal and devolved levels. 'They can be secured for Scotland's relationship with the rest of the UK now,' added Sir Menzies' report, 'allowing other constituent parts of the United Kingdom to adopt them should they choose to do so.'

Under the terms of the Edinburgh Agreement, the Scottish Parliament will lose the power to hold a referendum on independence at the end of 2014, although in any case the Scottish Government has repeatedly stated that it has no plans to push for another ballot for at least 'a generation' (which Nicola Sturgeon has defined as 15 years). Some Unionists have suggested that further devolution to Scotland would require a referendum across the whole UK, but if – as the experience in Quebec demonstrates – there is a NO vote in this referendum, another on independence seems likely at some point in the future.

12

Recommended Further Reading

Broun, Davuit, *Scottish Independence and the Idea of Britain: From the Picts to Alexander III*, Edinburgh University Press, Edinburgh, 2013.

Brown, Gordon, *My Scotland, Our Britain: A Future Worth Sharing*, Simon & Schuster, London, 2014.

Brown, Tom and McLeish, Henry, *Scotland: A Suitable Case for Treatment*, Luath Press, Edinburgh, 2009.

Bryan, Pauline and Kane, Tommy (eds.), *Class, Nation and Socialism: The Red Paper on Scotland 2014*, Glasgow Caledonian University Archives, Glasgow, 2013.

Bulmer, Elliot, *A Model Consitution for Scotland: Making Democracy Work*, Luath Press, Edinburgh, 2011.

Colley, Linda, *Acts of Union and Disunion*, Profile Books, London, 2013.

Foley, James and Ramand, Pete, *Yes: The Radical Case for Scottish Independence*, Pluto Press, London, 2014.

Gall, Gregor (ed.), *Scotland's Road to Socialism: Time to Choose*, Scottish Left Review Press, Glasgow, 2013.

Goudie, Andrew (ed.), *Scotland's Future: The Economics of Constitutional Change*, Dundee University Press, Dundee, 2013.

Gray, Alasdair, *Independence: An Argument for Home Rule*, Canongate, Edinburgh, 2014.

Hames, Scott (ed.), *Unstated: Writers on Scottish Independence*, Word Power Books, Edinburgh, 2012.

Hassan, Gerry and Mitchell, James, *After Independence*, Luath Press, Edinburgh, 2013.

Hassan, Gerry, *Caledonian Dreaming: The Quest for a Different Scotland*, Luath Press, Edinburgh, 2014.

Hassan, Gerry, *The Strange Death of Labour Scotland*,
    Edinburgh University Press, Edinburgh, 2012.

Keating, Michael and Harvey, Malcolm, *Small Nations in a
    Big World*, Luath Press, 2014

Keegan, William, *Britain without Oil: What Lies Ahead?*,
    Penguin, London, 1986.

Kerevan, George and Cochrane, Alan, *Scottish
    Independence: Yes or No (Great Debate)*, The History
    Press, Gloucestershire, 2014.

Lynch, Peter, *History of the Scottish National Party*, Welsh
    Academic Press, Cardiff, 1999.

Macwhirter, Iain, *Road to Referendum*, Cargo, Glasgow, 2013.

Marr, Andrew, *The Battle for Scotland*, Penguin, London,
    2013.

Maxwell, Stephen, *Arguing for Independence: Evidence,
    Risks and the Wicked Issues*, Luath Press, Edinburgh,
    2012.

Maxwell, Stephen, *The Case for Left Wing Nationalism:
    Essays and Articles*, Luath Press, Edinburgh, 2013.

McCrone, Gavin, *Scottish Independence: Weighing Up the
    Economics*, Birlinn, Edinburgh, 2014.

McLean, Iain, Lodge, Guy and Gallagher, Jim, *Scotland's
    Choices: The Referendum and What Happens
    Afterwards*, Edinburgh University Press, Edinburgh,
    2013.

McLeish, Henry, *Scotland: A Growing Divide: Old Nations,
    New Ideas*, Luath Press, Edinburgh, 2012.

Melding, David, *The Reformed Union: The UK as a
    Federation*, Institute of Welsh Affairs, Cardiff, 2013.

Mitchell, James, Bennie, Lyn and Johns, Rob, *The Scottish National Party: Transition to Power*, Oxford University Press, Oxford, 2012.

Mitchell, James, *The Scottish Question*, Oxford University Press, Oxford, 2014.

Moffat, Alexander and Riach, Alan, *Arts of Independence*, Luath Press, Edinburgh, 2014.

Nairn, Tom, *The Break-Up of Britain*, Verso Books, London, 1977.

Qvortrup, Matt, *Direct Democracy: A Comparative Study of the Theory and Practice of Government by the People*, Manchester University Press, Manchester, 2013.

Reid, Angus and Davis, Mary, *A Modest Proposal: For the Agreement of the People*, Luath Press, Edinburgh, 2014.

Riddoch, Lesley, *Blossom: What Scotland Needs to Flourish*, Luath Press, Edinburgh, 2013.

The Royal Society of Edinburgh, *Enlightening the Constitutional Debate*, The Royal Society of Edinburgh and the British Academy, Edinburgh, 2014.

Sillars, Jim, *In Place of Fear II: A Socialist Programme for an Independent Scotland*, Vagabond Voices, Glasgow, 2014.

The Scottish Government, *Scotland's Future: Your Guide to an Independent Scotland*, The Scottish Government, Edinburgh, 2013.

Torrance, David, *Alex Salmond: Against the Odds*, Birlinn, Edinburgh, 2009.

Torrance, David, *Britain Rebooted: Scotland in a Federal Union*, Luath Press, Edinburgh, 2014.

Torrance, David, *The Battle of Britain: Scotland and The Independence Referendum*, Biteback Publishing, Hull, 2013.

Torrance, David, *We in Scotland: Thatcherism in a Cold Climate*, Birlinn, Edinburgh, 2009.

Whatley, Christopher A., *The Scots and the Union: Then and Now*, Edinburgh University Press, Edinburgh, 2014.

Websites

news.bbc.co.uk/1/hi/scotland/6739007.stm

www.reformscotland.com/public/publications/scotlands
economic future.pdf

www.cpag.org.uk/scotland/child-poverty-facts-and-figures

www.scotland.gov.uk/Resource/0042/00428074.pdf

www.scottish.parliament.uk/S4_EconomyEnergyandTourism
Committee/Yes_Scotland.pdf

www.fivemillionquestions.org

Some other books published by **LUATH** PRESS

Britain Rebooted: Scotland in a Federal Union

David Torrance

ISBN: 978 1 910021 11 8 £7.99 PBK

Would federalism work in the UK?

Wouldn't England dominate a British federation?

How would powers be distributed between federal and Home Nation level?

What about the House of Lords?

In the run up to the historic referendum on Scottish independence there has been a plethora of tracts, articles and books arguing for and against, but there remains a gap in the literature: the case for Scotland becoming part of a 'rebooted' federal Union. It is an old, usually Liberal, dream, but one still worth fighting for.

It is often assumed that federalism is somehow 'alien' to the Scottish and British constitutional tradition but in this short book journalist David Torrance argues that not only has the UK already become a quasi-federal state but that formal federation is the best way of squaring the competing demands of Nationalists and Unionists.

He also uses Scotland's place within a federal UK to examine other potential reforms with a view to tackling ever-increasing inequality across the British Isles and create a more equal, successful and constitutionally coherent country.

Great Scottish Speeches

Introduced and Edited by David Torrance

Foreword by Alex Salmond

ISBN 978 1 906817 27 4 PBK £9.99

Some Great Scottish Speeches were the result of years of contemplation. Some flourished in heat of the moment. Whatever the background of the ideas expressed, the speeches not only provide a snapshot of their time, but express views that still resonate in Scotland today, whether you agree with the sentiments or not.

Encompassing speeches made by Scots or in Scotland, this carefully selected collection reveals the character of a nation. Themes of religion, independence and socialism cross paths with sporting encouragement, Irish Home Rule and Miss Jean Brodie.

Ranging from the legendary speech of the Caledonian chief Calgacus in 83AD right up to Alex Salmond's election victory in 2007, these are the speeches that created modern Scotland.

... what has not faded is the power of the written and spoken word – as this first-rate collection of Scottish speeches demonstrates.
PRESS AND JOURNAL

Arguing for Independence: Evidence, Risk and the Wicked Issues

Stephen Maxwell

ISBN: 978 1 908373 33 5 PBK £9.99

What sorts of arguments and evidence should carry the most weight in assessing the case for and against Scottish independence? Given the complexity of the question and the range of the possible consequences, can either side in the argument pretend to certainty, or must we simply be satisfied with probability or even plausibility? Are there criteria for sifting the competing claims and counter-claims and arriving at a rational decision on Scotland's future?

Stephen Maxwell, who was widely regarded as one Scotland's finest political thinkers, presents the case for Scottish independence under six main headings: the democratic case, the economic case, the social case, the international case, the cultural case and the environmental case. He concludes with a series of rebuttals to doubters under the heading 'Aye, But.'

Arguing for Independence is Stephen Maxwell's legacy to all who wish to make up their own minds on the independence debate.

A fine contribution by a fine man.
ALEX SALMOND

The Case for Left Wing Nationalism

Stephen Maxwell

ISBN: 978 1 908373 87 8 PBK £9.99

Spanning four politically and socially tumultuous decades, Stephen Maxwell's essays explore the origins and development of the Scottish Nationalist movement. As an instrumental member of the SNP, life-long activist and intellectual, Maxwell provides a unique insight into the debate over Scottish independence.

The Case for Left Wing Nationalism considers the class dynamics of the constitutional debate, deconstructs the myths that underpin Scottish political culture and exposes the role Scottish institutions have played and continue to play in restricting Scotland's progress.

In this wide-ranging analysis, Maxwell draws on a wealth of cultural, economic and historical sources. From debating the very nature of nationalism itself, to tackling the immediate social issues that Scotland faces, Maxwell establishes a very real picture of contemporary Scotland and its future.

It stands as a fine contribution by a fine man.
ALEX SALMOND

Blossom: What Scotland Needs to Flourish

Lesley Riddoch

ISBN: 978 1 908373 69 4 PBK £11.99

Weeding out vital components of Scottish identity from decades of political and social tangle is no mean task, but it's one journalist Lesley Riddoch has undertaken.

Dispensing with the tired, yo-yoing jousts over fiscal commissions, devo something-or-other and EU in-or-out, *Blossom* pinpoints both the buds of growth and the blight that's holding Scotland back. Drawing from its people and history, as well as the experience of the Nordic countries and the author's own passionate and outspoken perspective, this is a plain-speaking but incisive call to restore equality and control to local communities and let Scotland flourish.

Not so much an intervention in the independence debate as a heartfelt manifesto for a better democracy.
THE SCOTSMAN

Caledonian Dreaming: The Quest for a Different Scotland

Gerry Hassan

ISBN: 978 1 910021 32 3 UK £11.99

Caledonian Dreaming: The Quest for a Different Scotland offers a penetrating and original way forward for Scotland beyond the current independence debate. It identifies the myths of modern Scotland, describes what they say and why they need to be seen as myths. Hassan argues that Scotland is already changing, as traditional institutions and power decline and new forces emerge, and outlines a prospectus for Scotland to become more democratic and to embrace radical and far-reaching change.

Hassan drills down to deeper reasons why the many dysfunctions of British democracy could dog an independent Scotland too. With a non-partisan but beady eye on society both sides of the border, in this clever book here are tougher questions to consider than a mere Yes/No.
POLLY TOYNBEE, writer and journalist, *The Guardian*

A brilliant book unpacking the political narratives that have shaped modern Scotland in order to create a space to imagine anew. A book about Scotland important to anyone, anywhere, dreaming a new world.
STEPHEN DUNCOMBE, author

Scotland: The Road Divides

Henry McLeish and Tom Brown

ISBN: 978 1 906307 24 0 PBK £8.99

The Brown government must engage with the Scottish question while at the same time, ceding yet more British sovereignty to the European Union... it is here that the interests of the English and the other nationalities of the UK divide.

FRANK FIELD, MP

[This paper] *is the first step in a national conversation.*

UK GOVERNMENT GREEN PAPER 2007 'THE GOVERNANCE OF BRITAIN'

This paper is the first step in a wide-ranging national conversation about the future of Scotland.

SCOTTISH GOVERNMENT WHITE PAPER 2007 'CHOOSING SCOTLAND'S FUTURE'

This book aims to take these conversations forward, to engage in the key issues facing Scotland and the UK.

A hard-hitting, incisive and informed look at where the devolution journey has taken us – from the heady days of the new Blair government in 1997 to the dramatic events of 2007 – and where we go from here.

Small Nations in a Big World

Michael Keating and Malcolm Harvey

ISBN: 978 1 910021 20 0 PBK £9.99

Small northern European nations have been a major point of reference in the Scottish independence debate. For nationalists, they have been an 'arc of prosperity' while in the aftermath of the financial crash, unionists lampooned the 'arc of insolvency'. Both characterisations are equally misleading. Small nations can do well in the global marketplace, yet they face the world in very different ways. Some accept market logic and take the 'low road' of low wages, low taxes and light regulation, with a correspondingly low level of public services. Others take the 'high road' of social investment, which entails a larger public sector and higher taxes. Such a strategy requires innovative government, flexibility and social partnership.

Keating and Harvey compare the experience of the Nordic and Baltic states and Ireland, which have taken very different roads and ask what lessons can be learnt for Scotland. They conclude that an independent nation is possible but that hard choices would need to be taken.

Luath Press Limited

committed to publishing well written books worth reading

LUATH PRESS takes its name from Robert Burns, whose little collie Luath (*Gael.*, swift or nimble) tripped up Jean Armour at a wedding and gave him the chance to speak to the woman who was to be his wife and the abiding love of his life. Burns called one of 'The Twa Dogs' Luath after Cuchullin's hunting dog in Ossian's *Fingal*. Luath Press was established in 1981 in the heart of Burns country, and now resides a few steps up the road from Burns' first lodgings on Edinburgh's Royal Mile.

Luath offers you distinctive writing with a hint of unexpected pleasures.

Most bookshops in the UK, the US, Canada, Australia, New Zealand and parts of Europe either carry our books in stock or can order them for you. To order direct from us, please send a £sterling cheque, postal order, international money order or your credit card details (number, address of cardholder and expiry date) to us at the address below. Please add post and packing as follows: UK – £1.00 per delivery address; overseas surface mail – £2.50 per delivery address; overseas airmail – £3.50 for the first book to each delivery address, plus £1.00 for each additional book by airmail to the same address. If your order is a gift, we will happily enclose your card or message at no extra charge.

Luath Press Limited
543/2 Castlehill
The Royal Mile
Edinburgh EH1 2ND
Scotland
Telephone: 0131 225 4326 (24 hours)
Fax: 0131 225 4324
email: sales@luath.co.uk
Website: www.luath.co.uk